FOOD SERVICE
MENUS

*Pricing and Managing The Food Service
Menu For Maximum Profit*

By Lora Arduser

The Food Service Professional's Guide To:
Food Service Menus Pricing and Managing The Food Service Menu For Maximum Profit: 365 Secrets Revealed

Atlantic Publishing Group, Inc. Copyright © 2003
1210 SW 23rd Place • Ocala, Florida 34474
800-814-1132 • FAX 352-622-5836

www.atlantic-pub.com • e-mail: sales@atlantic-pub.com

SAN Number :268-1250

ISBN-10: 0-910627-23-1
ISBN-13: 978-0-910627-23-8

Library of Congress Cataloging-in-Publication Data

Brown, Douglas Robert, 1960-
Pricing and managing your food service menu for maximum profit : 365 secrets revealed / by Douglas Robert Brown.
p. cm. -- (The food service professionals guide to ; 13)
Includes bibliographical references and index.
ISBN 0-910627-23-1 (pbk. : alk. paper)
1. Food service--Prices. 2. Restaurants--Prices. 3. Menus.
I. Title. II. Series.
TX911.3.P7B76 2003
647.95'068'1--dc21

2002011171

10 9 8 7 6 5 4 3 2

Printed in the United States

Cover and interior design by Meg Buchner • megadesn@mchsi.com

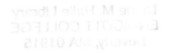

CONTENTS

MARKETING YOUR MENU (& YOUR RESTAURANT)

OPERATIONAL CONTROLS & MENU MANAGEMENT

FINAL TASKS

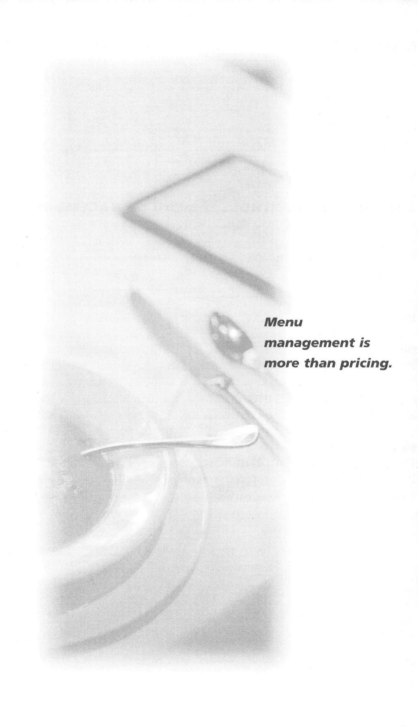

Menu management is more than pricing.

INTRODUCTION

Menu management is an important component of profit realization in the restaurant industry. Just you manage your employees, you should manage ır menu in order to control costs and increase sales rease profit. Too many restaurant managers leave nu design decisions to printers, or they simply do t devote enough time and expense to their menu velopment.

ıen pricing menu items you do need to take food cost, or and operating expenses into account, but you o have to be aware of what the customer is willing pay, what the competition is charging and what your ablishment offers in comparison to the competition. e bottom line is that your prices have to cover your sts plus provide a profit. If this doesn't happen, you ı't stay in business. And while menu management ıy be perplexing, it isn't brain surgery! Using the tools cussed in this book, you will be able to manage your :nu so that you'll see maximum profits.

:nu management entails more than making pricing :isions: putting high prices on items to realize : greatest profits or putting low prices on items to :rease sales is not always the best way to increase ır profits. Granted, that strategy may work in the ort term, but to generate profits consistently for your ablishment, you need to have a menu program in ıce. This program will include making your menu part your marketing plan, finding ways to lower costs,

putting purchasing and production controls in place, a
well as managing of your employees.

And while there are many factors to consider in
developing, pricing and managing your menu, it's an
easy, often overlooked way to increase profits. The
following pages will provide simple, easy-to-implement
tools that you can start using today to increase your
profits.

CHAPTER ONE

GETTING STARTED

ho Are You?

s a food service manager, you make decisions every day. But, one of the more perplexing decisions you ake is what to put on your menu and what prices to arge. While it may seem that it should be a simple, alitative exercise, many quantitative factors go into e price decision-making process. Before you can begin aking pricing decisions, you have to establish the enu. To do this, you must have a clear idea of what ur establishment is and what identity you want to oject to your customers.

- **Feasibility study.** While you probably know the type of food establishment you want to manage or own, before sinking your money into a particular identity, do a feasibility study in order to be sure your identity has a market in the location of your establishment. Make sure that the type of restaurant you want to manage and the type of food that you want to serve will be valued by your potential customers.

- **Where are your customers coming from and what do they want?** Are they looking for a quick lunch before heading out for a noon walk? Or, are they looking for a place to celebrate family birthdays? Restaurants and catering establish-ments are located at all kinds of spots. They are in strip malls, industrial areas, suburbs and urban settings. Where is your restaurant located? A prime city spot? A mall?

- **Ask yourself the following basic questions:** Answering these types of questions will help you define your objectives and identity your potential clientele. It will also help you develop, price and manage your menu:

  - Are you a full-service buffet, fast-food restaurant or catering operation?

  - Is your main business at breakfast, lunch or dinner?

  - How is your restaurant decorated?

  - Do you serve alcohol?

  - Do you use china and white tablecloths, or plastic ware and paper napkins?

  - Who do you see as a typical customer? Families? Two-income couples? Seniors?

  - Do people come to pick up a quick dinner to take home, or are your customers more likely to eat at your establishment for a special occasion?

  - Do you have a limited menu or an extensive menu?

ustomer Profile

What are the local demographics of the area in which your establishment is located? According a National Restaurant Association survey (2001), ouseholds with an annual gross income of $15,000 $19,999 spend 34 percent of their food budgets on ning out. The same study concluded that people under te age of 25 spend 45.5 percent of their food budgets ning out. When analyzing your customer profile, take Ivantage of information like this. Spend some time searching industry publications to help you define our average customer and their food-spending charac- ristics. Consider the following:

- **Target market.** Before you create or change your menu and pricing, you need to analyze your potential customers in your target market. Key considerations include:
  - What is the age breakdown?
  - The number of households?
  - Average family income?
  - Average family size?
  - Average education?

- **Suburban sector.** If you are located in a suburban setting and your customer profile is a family of four that earns between $60,000 and $80,000 a year, you would probably do well as a mid-price family restaurant.

- **Urban sector.** Is your establishment located in a business and/or entertainment urban area? If so, investigate the following:
  - What types of businesses are there?

  - How many businesses are there?

  - What are their hours of operation?

  - Are there entertainment venues near?

  - How many and of what type?

- **Business menus.** If you are located in a business district, what are the hours of these businesses' operations? This information will help you determine what to include on your menu and how to price it. Include higher-end entrées for business lunches and dinners. People who are dining their clients are often out to impress, so you would want to strive for an upscale environment featuring a wine list and more expensive entrées than you might find at a family restaurant. Whether or not businesses are located in your target market area will also help you determine your hours of operation and which meals to serve.

The Competition

You need to know your competition as well as your customer. Find out what other establishments exist in your market and which ones are marketing the same segment of the population as you are.

- **Study the menus of the competition.** Find out what they are selling and for how much. If Joe's Steak is selling a 10-oz strip steak for $12.95 and you are selling the same item at $17.95, you can be pretty sure the customers are going to buy it from Joe's. If you do something special with the strip steak or the ambiance of your restaurant is much nicer than Joe's, then this may allow you to charge more.

- **Become a secret shopper.** An easy (and fun) way to find out what the competition is up to is to be a "secret shopper." Go to your competitors and eat at their restaurants. Many may even have a carryout menu you can take with you.

- **Get chatting to potential clients in the neighborhood.** Most people have useful (and strong) opinions about what they want to see on a menu in their local food service outlets. People who have lived in the neighborhood for many years are likely to know what would work for your establishment.

velop a Market Survey

he easiest way to compile and interpret information on potential customers and competition is by veloping a market survey. The following examples n be used as a guide for how to set up a survey. The ormation you need to complete these sheets usually n be found in records at the public library, city offices d the chamber of commerce. Small business associa-ns can also provide you with a wealth of information. ructure your survey along the following lines:

MARKET SURVEY — Potential Customers

1. Approximate total population of target market area _____

2. Number of households _____

3. Average household size _____

4. Ages

        18–24 _____%
        25–34 _____%
        35–50 _____%
        51–64 _____%
        65–up _____%

5. Household Annual Incomes

        Below $11,000   _____%
        $11,000–23,999   _____%
        $24,000–35,999   _____%
        $36,000–49,999   _____%
        $50,000–79,999   _____%
        $80,000–$100,000 _____%
        above $100,000   _____%

The following sheet can be used for each competitor:

COMPETITION SURVEY

Competitor Name _____

Location _____

What are the major roads in vicinity? _____

Is there a sign? _____

Is there parking?_____

Are they on a bus line or near other public transportation? _____

What is the general appearance of the building exterior? _____

_____

_____

What is the general appearance of the building interior?_____

_____

_____

Describe the dining areas (booths or tables, type of table clothes, etc.). _____

_____

_____

_____

What days and hours are they open? _____

They serve: ❑ Breakfast   ❑ Lunch   ❑ Dinner

They offer: ❑ Carryout   ❑ Delivery   ❑ Catering

Do they serve alcohol?   ❑ Yes   ❑ No

What's the seating capacity?_____

What type of cuisine do they serve? _____

How quickly do they turn over tables?_____

What would you guess the average guest check total is? _____

Do they offer entertainment? _____

What are the price ranges of appetizers? _____

Entrées?_____ Desserts? _____

The Feasibility Study

The second step is to turn your attention to your establishment. A feasibility study looks at your business and analyzes its ability to be successful and profitable. A feasibility study can help pull all this information together. In order to make a profit in your restaurant, you must know what prices to charge. Consider the following:

- **Costs to include in your feasibility study.** Che out basic costs for items such as linen, employee uniforms, equipment, china, insurance, utility bills, rent or mortgage, office supplies, payroll expenses, taxes, advertising expenses, repair and maintenance expenses, food cost, wages, health insurance and workers' compensation expenses.

- **Overview.** Summarize the information you have gathered so far. The information about costs, alor with the general sales information that you've already acquired, will help you get a good picture of your restaurant's health. It will also help you determine what prices you will need to charge to remain in operation, at a profit.

- **Help with feasibility studies.** The National Restaurant Association has sample feasibility studies that may be helpful in creating your own To obtain information on this, membership, or other issues, you can visit their Web site at www. restaurant.org, or write to:

National Restaurant Association
1200 17th St NW
Washington, D.C. 20036
202-331-5960

w Your Menu Fits into Your Overall Marketing
ategy

ou've done your homework. You know your
objectives as a food service establishment, your
ential customers and your competition. Now it's
e to put this information to work for you. All the
rmation you gathered doing a market survey and
sibility study can be used to develop and manage
r menu.

- **Identity.** Design a menu that will fit your restaurant's identity, but one that is, nevertheless, viable in your market. By knowing the type of customers you can expect and what works and doesn't work for your competition, you can design your menu for maximum effect. By identifying your market and your operation, you have taken the first step in establishing a menu price range.

- **The restaurant menu itself is an important internal marketing tool.** A well-designed menu can attract a customer's attention to specific items and increase the chances that the customer will purchase those items and this can impact your check averages and profits. For instance, if you put an item in a box on the menu, the customer's eye will be drawn to this area of the menu (they can't buy it if they don't see it!). It can help you achieve your profit goals to feature higher profit items.

- **Reinforce your unique identity.** Incorporate the menu design into business cards, signs, table tents, stationery and logos to provide a cohesive marketing package.

Communicate Your Establishment's Image

The menu is the one thing your customer will read. Because of this, it is an excellent device to communicate the restaurant's image. It should complement the décor, service style, price range and type of cuisine. When the customer looks at the menu everything should be working to communicate the restaurant's personality. The customer should be able to sense this from the types of items on the menu to the type style in which the items are printed. When developing a menu marketing strategy, four marketing factors come into play: product, promotion, place and price. These variables can be manipulated to achieve goals, such as lowering food cost and raising profit margins.

- **Product.** This refers to the item that you are selling. Some of the components of the product include portion size, presentation and the placement of the item on your menu. If you are a catering operation, product also refers to other services that you provide, such as floral displays or entertainment. Here are some examples of way that you can adjust your product to create large profits:
    - Decrease the portion size of a particular menu item.

    - Increase the portion size and the price of an item.

    - Add side items and increase your price.

- **Promotion.** This covers anything that is done to draw attention to menu selections. This may be table tents, menu clip-ons, graphics, etc. Here a some examples of ways that promotions can be used to create larger profits:

- Use table tents to promote a menu item that isn't selling well.

- As customers are waiting to be seated, have a server come around with an appetizer sampler plate, enticing customers to order appetizers while they wait or after they are seated.

- **Place.** This refers to where the customer gets the food. Do you have table service? A drive-through? Delivery service? Do you offer on-site or off-site catering? Here are some examples of ways that place can be used to create larger profits:

  - Consider upgrading your service style. If you do, you may be able to upgrade prices as well.

  - Consider adding delivery service or carryout to increase your sales.

- **Price.** The price you charge will influence what a customer chooses to purchase. Low prices, however, are not always the best way to build a customer base. You need to look at your restaurant's style and determine if low or discounted prices are likely to entice the customers you are seeking or drive them away. Price should reflect three things: your costs, your desired profit and what the customer will pay. Here is an example of how price can be used to create larger profits:

  - On a night that is usually slow for your establishment, start to offer a reduced price to draw customers. You could offer an "early bird" special, or perhaps some percentage off particular entrées on that night only.

Make sure the type of menu suits your restaurant.

CHAPTER TWO

MENU DEVELOPMENT

nu Styles

Menu styles can be described in terms of how much or how little variety they offer. Things that may ermine whether you offer a limited or extensive menu lude kitchen size and labor cost control. Menus h more options, however, do have a broader appeal l may help keep your regular customers happy providing them with enough interesting alterna- es to keep them coming back. Limited menus allow taurants to keep products simple and keep a tight n on food and labor costs. These menus may offer items or few ways to prepare items. Extensive nus (like the ones you see in Chinese and Mexican taurants) may use a small number of ingredients l simply prepare them in numerous ways. On the er hand, there may be a wide variety of ingredients ered on the menu as well. These types of menus are en found in finer-dining establishments. Consider the owing:

- **Opt for the type of menu that best suits your establishment.** There are advantages to both menu styles. The main advantages of limited menus are lower purchasing, production and service costs. Having lower costs means you can charge lower prices, so it could increase profits by increasing sales, appealing to customers who value a low menu price. Extensive menus have

the advantage of having broader customer appea
Also, while you will have higher costs, you can
charge higher prices. Higher profits can be reali
because you can charge these prices and becaus
you will have an increased customer base. Choo
what's right for you.

- **Limited resources?** For example, if you have a
  small kitchen or a staff that is not highly skilled,
  you may want to limit the number of items you o
  Remember, it's quality, not quantity, that counts!

- **Skilled chefs at your disposal?** Introduce a wid
  range of ingredients and dishes only if you have
  the infrastructure to do so. You'll need to emplo:
  skilled labor and also be able to offer an elegant
  dining environment for this type of menu to yiel
  maximum profits.

- **Variety.** So, how many menu items should you
  offer? A good general guideline is to base your
  decision upon your restaurant's identity, your
  kitchen staff's skills and your target food cost. C
  course you want to be able to provide the custor
  with some variety, but not at the expense of
  controlling inventory and costs, and certainly no
  at the risk of overtaxing your production or serv
  staffs.

- **Expand your menu.** Making some changes in
  your menu style can mean increased profits. Foi
  instance, fast-food restaurants, traditionally, ha\
  offered limited menus. In today's market, howev
  these establishments are expanding their menus
  in order to expand their customer base. If you
  manage a fast-food restaurant, expanding your
  menu is one way to increase profits. Consider
  adding some new sides or desserts to your existi
  menu.

- **Hire a skilled chef.** One of the quickest ways to expand your menu and increase profits is to hire a skilled chef. By employing staff with greater culinary skills, you can increase your menu offerings and provide items that may look and taste better. Sure, a coveted chef will command a higher wage, but if you keep this in mind when restructuring your profit margins, you'll be able to cover these costs. By providing your customer with higher-quality food, you may also be able to increase your prices. Draw in new customers - increase profitability.

er a limited Menu - Increase Table Turnover

you aren't interested in expanding your menu, but
ou still want to realize greater profits, you can do it
h a limited menu offering. One way is by increasing
le turnover. Most fast-food and lower-priced
taurants depend on quick turnover to realize a profit.
help speed up the ordering and eating process, try a
of the following ideas:

- **Keep your menu descriptions short.** This will speed up the time it takes customers to read your menu and decide what to order.

- **Have places for the customer to put trays and garbage.** If customers clean up their tables, it saves your employees time in getting tables ready for the next customers.

- **Ambiance.** The atmosphere around your customers will help determine if the meal pace feels slow or quick. If you have piped-in music, keep the tempo upbeat. Keep the colors of your restaurant bright, as this also makes a difference in how the customer perceives the established pace.

- **Use plastic and paper products rather than glass for serving.** Paper products are synonymo with fast food and save on dishwashing labor.

Types of Menus

Menus can be arranged in a number of ways. The types of meals that they present may classify the breakfast menus, lunch menus and dinner menus. They can also be classified by how they price items. Menus can also be classified by the type of food servic that uses them: institutional, industrial, commercial, entertainment, etc. Different types of operations usual have particular formats in general use. First familiariz yourself with the following basic terms:

- **Á la carte menus** price everything separately, including salads and side orders.

- **Semi-á la carte menus** usually include a side (such as a vegetable and potato) and a salad witl the main entrée, but they price soups, desserts and appetizers separately.

- **Prix fixe menus** offer a complete meal at a set price. This may include an appetizer, entrée and dessert, or it can be a five-course meal.

- **Fixed menus don't change.** When new menus are printed, the only thing that usually changes is price

- **Seasonal menus** take advantage of the season, allowing the establishment to use the freshest ingredients possible. They also allow the chef or kitchen staff more creativity. Seasonal menus m: help lower food cost by using seasonally availabl goods.

- **Verbal menus** are sometimes used by fine-dining restaurants, and may supplement a printed menu. Many restaurants have their servers verbally explain the specials, which also allows for suggestive selling. If you choose only to use a verbal menu, the staff must be well trained for it to work.

fine Your Style

Armed with your customer profile, decide which of these pricing styles is most appropriate for your staurant. If you are a family restaurant, you will obably scare customers away if you offer prix fixe icing. Alternatively, if your main business comes from nch, you may want to consider using á la carte pricing cause this allows the customer to order smaller nounts. Since most people save their big meal of the y for dinner, your lunch patrons will appreciate this xibility and you are likely to attract return, and new, siness.

- **Tips for compiling an institutional-type menu.** Keep in mind that a different set of rules applies when it comes to institutions, such as schools, colleges, hospitals, correctional facilities and nursing homes. These establishments often use cycle menus. A cycle is written for a specific period of time until it repeats its first offering. The same menu is always served on the same day of the week in a typical cycle menu. Remember, any divergence from this pattern can seriously dent profitability.

- **Can you offer a cycle menu that is imaginative?** Yes, the scope is greater than you think. For example, a cycle menu can reflect ingredient seasonality and holiday fare. For

more information on menu management in instit
tional situations, visit the following Web sites:

American School Food Service Association
www.asfa.org

**National Association of College and
University Food Services**
www.nacufs.org

**American Society for Healthcare
Food Service Administrators**
www.ashfsa.org

- **Commercial operations have the widest
  selection of menu types available to them.**
  If you are compiling a menu for a commercial
  establishment, flexibility is the name of the game
  Use any of the pricing mixes mentioned above.
  They may have separate breakfast, lunch and
  dinner menus. They may even use a cycle menu.
  The most common formats found in commercial
  food service establishments, however, are the
  fixed menu and the seasonal menu. The scope
  for creating imaginative menus, in this sector, is
  immense.

- **Special-function menus.** Although these types
  of menus are used by restaurants and caterers
  for special events, such as wedding receptions or
  banquets, they are designed to reflect the wants
  the particular customer and do offer considerabl
  scope. Develop a series of menus for customers t
  choose from. Try offering several entrées, salads,
  vegetables and desserts for them to combine in a
  way that satisfies their budget and taste.

- **Thinking of making major menu changes?** If
  you want to add items or categories, you may
  want to consider using a seasonal menu. This

will allow you to experiment and see what works and what doesn't. An inn in Midway, Kentucky, called The Holly Hill Inn, for instance, varied their menu every month after the new owners began to operate. Each month they offered a different theme, such as Italian fare or Asian. This allowed the owners to identify the cuisine they wanted to put forward as part of their identity and it also allowed them to train their kitchen staff in various preparation methods.

- **Make the most of industrial-type menus.** Bear in mind that industrial institution restaurants have the advantage of serving a largely "captive" audience, such as the employees of large corporations or factories. While these food outlets may not be profitable in the truest sense of the word, selling at a break-even point, they are basically still run like commercial food service operations - and at least you can guarantee a steady flow of customers. Listen to their preferences.

tering Establishment Menus

Vhile catering menus have the same function as restaurant menus – to lead customers to buy e meal service that is most profitable to you and :ases them at the same time – there are a significant fferences with catering menus. Many food service anagers are employed by operations that do only tering or by restaurants that specifically offer catering one of their services. Catering facilities do raise some ecial issues when it comes to menu pricing and menu anagement. Consider the following:

- **Menu presentation.** Make sure that your catering menu has an eye-catching design. Remember, menu choices at a restaurant are made by the individual diner, whereas catering menus are normally decided upon by several people. Catering menus are often reviewed in customers' own homes or offices, prior to their meeting with any food service personnel. The customer is also likely to be reviewing menus from several different operations at the same time. Because of this, the appearance of the catering menu takes on even greater significance as a marketing and communication tool.

- **Menu cover.** The design format of catering menus is often determined by the sales presentation cover. This is important - the menu is, in effect, part of a sales package. A proven winning formula is to produce a menu with an overall dimension of 9 inches by 12 inches - simply because this size easily fits into a business envelope. The most common format is two panel with pockets.

- **Content.** Always opt for broad appeal, with the emphasis upon traditional dishes, together with a few dashes of inspiration.

Catering Menu Pricing

Pricing for catering menus has always been a sensitive issue when it comes to staff tolerance levels. Don't be greedy and lose a massive contract. Think long-term

- **Pricing structure.** As a general guideline, adopt one of the following tried-and-tested pricing structures for your catering menu:
  - Fixed price (table d'hôte or prix fixe)

  - Mixed pricing (semi-á la carte)

- Individual course pricing (á la carte)

- **Where do I start?** Here are a few examples to get you going. Adapt, add and delete according to the preferences of your customers.

xed Pricing

.is includes all menu items and gives a price per rson:

> Cedar planked salmon on herbed lentil couscous
> Roast pork tenderloin with a port maple sauce
> Mixed green salad with orange vinaigrette
> Roasted green beans
> Whipped sweet potatoes
> Pumpkin crème brûlée
> **$37.00 per person**

xed Pricing

.th mixed pricing, the customer gets a set price th the option of changing different courses for an ditional charge per person:

> **Appetizers** . . . .**Please add $3.50 per guest**
> Cedar planked salmon on herbed lentil couscous
> Blue cheese baklava
> Gougere
> Lobster spring rolls with basil oil
> Raspberry and brie phyllo cups
>
> **Desserts** . . . .**Please add $4.75 per guest**
> Flourless chocolate cake with raspberry coulis
> Pumpkin crème brûlée
> Gingered pear tart
> Passion fruit sorbet with coconut tuiles

Individual course pricing offers each menu item as a separate item with a separate per-person price:

Entrées (choose 1)

Cedar planked Copper River salmon $19.95

Filet mignon with Gorgonzola butter sauce $16.95

Seared duck breast with fig compote. $22.95

Salads (choose 1)

Arugula and mixed green salad
with orange vinaigrette $2.50

Wilted spinach with warm honey vinaigrette. $2.25

Pear and Maytag blue cheese with port vinaigrette . .$3.25

Vegetables (choose 1)

Braised bok choy $1.50

Grilled green beans with sun-dried tomato sauce . $2.00

Roasted asparagus with lemon and
Parmigiano-Reggiano. $3.50

Starch (choose 1)

Polenta triangles $3.00

Sweet potato latkes $3.25

Roasted new potatoes with rosemary $3.00

Dessert (choose 1)

Espresso crème brûlée $7.00

Raspberry mocha torte. $8.75

Key lime cake with homemade coconut ice cream. $8.25

Package pricing

To make the caterer's life easier, consider this simplifie option. Catering operations may do package pricing as well. A package price would give the customer a per-person price that includes food, beverage, entertainme and flowers.

- **Price range.** When offering your customer several different menus to choose from, make sure that your price range between menus falls within the $12-$15 band. A choice between menus that are priced at $18 and menus that are priced at $50 is too great a range.

w Adding Catering Can Help Increase Profits

*M*any restaurants offer on-site (and off-site) catering. The preceding menu examples can be used for sinesses solely engaged in catering or by restaurants at offer catering. Consider the following opportunities:

- **"Slow" nights.** Many restaurants close on Mondays and/or Tuesdays, because these nights tend to be slow and it would cost more to operate on those evenings than the restaurant would gain in sales. Use those nights for catered events. For a small increase in food and labor cost, you can make a significant increase in sales for the week.

- **Leftover inventory.** Create catering menus that allow you to use products on hand. When creating a catering menu, take the opportunity to include items that will allow you to use leftover inventory.

- **Current trends.** There several trends in catering that you may want to be aware of when designing menus for events. Investigate some of the possibilities.

- **Themed events.** These may be tied into an occasion that is being celebrated or some more generic theme, like a tropical buffet.

- **Stations.** For a stationed event, you'll need to set up several serving areas and offer a different cuisine at each. Often, ethnic cuisines are used f these: one station may be Italian, while the secon is Chinese and a third is a dessert station.

- **Hands-on parties.** These events let people participate in the food preparation. These are rur in a way similar to that of a hands-on cooking class.

- **Corporate events.** Consider marketing yourself t companies for corporate team-building sessions. In these sessions, groups of coworkers are put together to work as a team in a food production exercise.

- **Promotion**. Catering is a great way to advertise and promote your restaurant. But, you have to promote your catering side as well. Use your restaurant to promote your catering. Set up table tents or signs that let your customers know that you cater. Provide carryout-catering menus at the cashier or hostess station as well.

- **Advertise.** Use a rubber stamp on outgoing mail, saying, "We cater!"

Formatting Your Menu

We've looked at styles of menus you can use; now i time to decide what items will go on your menu. I you are fine-tuning an existing menu you will already have groups and categories. In fact, you may even kno specifically the dishes that you want to incorporate. However, if you are opening a business or are complet redoing your menu, you can get a handle on where to gin by working from general to specific.

- **Menu groups.** First things first. Decide what menu groups you will offer. Groups are: appetizers, entrées, soups, desserts, etc.

- **Next, decide what categories to offer within these groups.** For entrée choices, for instance, you could offer the following categories: beef, poultry, seafood, pork, vegetarian, lamb and veal. Then you must decide how many dishes you will offer in each category. You may have four beef dishes, three seafood, two poultry and one vegetarian, for example.

- **Finally, you must decide on the dishes themselves.** There are numerous recipe sources that you can call upon. Buy cookbooks and experiment with recipes you find there. Get online and look for recipes; there are hundreds, if not thousands, of useful sites! And don't forget to use the creativity of yourself and your kitchen staff!

- **As you create your menu, think about what you want to say.** What do you want to communicate to your customer? Make decisions about the categories to use, what to call different dishes and how many dishes to have.

- **Resources.** Think about the size of your kitchen and the skills of your staff. If your kitchen is small, you may want to limit the number of items you place on the menu. If you have a schooled and highly skilled kitchen staff, you may be able to prepare a greater number and variety of dishes.

Daily Specials

Many restaurants offer specials in addition to their regular menu. These specials are often hand-written on a board that can be seen as the customer enters the restaurant. Specials can also be written on inserts that are included with your regular printed menu. Or your servers can communicate them to the customers verbally.

- **Can specials offer you an opportunity to increase profits?** Yes! Do you regularly have leftovers? Is your inventory control a little slack? Solve the problem by offering specials. It's the perfect way to use up those extra products and eliminate cost from waste. If you have leftover chopped vegetables, you could make minestrone soup for the next day's soup du jour. Or, if you ordered too many chicken breasts, make grilled chicken breast sandwiches the next day's lunch special.

- **Specials may also be a good idea if you have a regular customer base.** Offering a changing repertoire will provide your regulars with some additional choices. This variety will help to keep them interested. Encourage them to return to your establishment rather than disappear to a new restaurant for something different.

- **New dishes.** Specials are also a good way to try out those new dishes that you're considering adding to the menu as regular items. Keep a tally of which dishes are the most popular. It will give you a clearer idea of which ones would be successful on your menu.

- **A word of caution about specials.** While developing these items may feed your kitchen staff's creative urge, make sure you have final approval on specials. Otherwise, they may impact food costs negatively if you have an overzealous cook or chef, or you may end up serving subquality food.

nk Menus

lcohol is a high-profit restaurant item. You may want to print a separate drink or wine menu. You use the menu to advertise unique or specialty nks. Know your customer and keep your eye on ds to determine whether or not your drink sales tify the cost of creating a separate menu. Investigate following possibilities:

- **Wine list.** You may want to consider adding a wine list and even a wine retail store. Offer the wines from the store on your menu.

- **Add a separate wine list.** This helps to upgrade your restaurant. People may see it as more of a special-occasion place and be willing to come for celebrations. They'll probably also be willing to spend more money than on just a regular night out.

- **Sell wine and increase profits.** Margins on wine are notoriously high. You may be able to increase your menu prices because of the increased value you are giving your customers!

- **A good way to increase your wine sales is by offering "tasters."** If a customer isn't sure which wine to choose, let him or her have a taste. By doing this, you make your customer feel special. It's fairly certain that once you do this, the customer will order the glass of wine. In addition other patrons at the same table are also likely to purchase wine at this point.

- **Product knowledge.** Make sure that your server are familiar with the items on your wine or specialty drinks lists. With a wine list, servers need to be well versed in "wine language" includi which types of wines go well with different dishe: In fact, you may want to include that informatioi on your menu. At the end of each menu item description, include the establishment's wine recommendations.

- **Wine tasting session.** Invite a wine vendor or a representative from a local wine shop to set up a tasting session for your employees. If your customers are wine connoisseurs, they'll certainl expect your staff to be knowledgeable about the products they're serving. Also, diners who may be a little intimated by wine are more likely to order a bottle if a server can make some suitable suggestions.

- **Ask vendors to provide you with fact sheets o specific wines.** They often have free table tents ; well as other promotional materials that they cai give to you. For more information on wines, try t following books:

  - *Exploring Wine: The Culinary Institute of America's Complete Guide to Wines of the Wor*

  - *Robert Parker's Buying Guide*

- Oz Clarke's *New Atlas of Wine*

- Hugh Johnson's *The World Atlas of Wine*

Most of these books and more are available at www.atlantic-pub.com.

There are also several good wine magazines, including:

Wine Spectator
www.winespectator.com/Wine/Home

Wine and Spirits
www.wineandspiritsmagazine.com

Wine Enthusiast
www.wineenthusiastmag.com

Sante
www.santemagazine.com

- **Computer software.** Explore the many computer software programs available nowadays. These programs can assist you with purchasing, tracking and pricing wines. One of these, called Clarifye, is available at www.claretsoftware.com. There are various service packages to choose from.

ildren's Menus

Children have a large influence on where the family dines. To gain the customer loyalty of children d their families, you must create a kid-friendly vironment. The main way to achieve this is to roduce a children's menu. Here are ten things to sider when developing a children's menu:

1. **Target age group.** Children aged 3 to 12 generally use kids' menus. However, make sur that you include items that all age groups will enjoy.

2. **Please the parents.** Make sure you offer items that will please the parents as well as the kids

3. **Use existing inventory.** Include items on the children's menu that are made from ingredient already in your inventory. This will help keep food costs down.

4. **Make the menu fun!** Use interesting names fc your menu items. Maybe create a theme for yo menu. You could do a pirate or animal theme, for instance. Gear artwork and text for childrer Use pictures and don't use fancy terms or fore words to describe the items.

5. **Budget items.** Remember, parents are looking for prices that fit their budgets. They also wan menu items that their children like to eat. Pric your menu accordingly. Some restaurants go a far as to let children under 12 eat for free whe dining with an adult.

6. **Games.** Create a menu that has games to occu the kids while they wait to be served. You may want to have puzzles or coloring activities on t menus to keep them busy.

7. **Make the food fun to eat.** For instance, Murphin Ridge Inn, a country inn in Adams County, Ohio, arranges the fruit on their kids' fruit plate in a smiley face.

8. **Offer a free dessert to kids.**

9.   **Have no-spill cups for the smaller kids to use.**

10. **The best way to determine what to put on your children's menu is to ask kids!** If you are a parent or you know someone with children, watch what they eat and find out what they are interested in. Do some research and find out the latest fad. Is it dinosaurs? Then use pictures of dinosaurs on your menu. But be careful. While graphics and games can be trendy, children's food should not. Kids are willing to try something new when they eat, but in general they are more comfortable with items that they know and love.

nu Design Software

ith the advent of the personal computer, there have been several menu-design software programs eloped specifically for the catering market. The initial t of the software will be recouped easily, as you will e on design and printing costs.

- **Build a template incorporating your establishment's logo.** The software is generally very easy to use, with built in templates, artwork, etc. Your finalized menus, with logos, can be printed out on a laser printer. Color, clip art, photos, artwork and graphics may be added.

- **Use the software to produce table tents and other promotional material.** Use your imagination.

- **Make changes easily.** Because you have control over the design process, changes can be made instantly. Daily menus can also be made, which is

a great way to accommodate any special purchas
that might have been made. Also, this allows for
instant price changes to reflect market condition
One such software program is MenuPro™. An
extensive demonstration of the software may be
found at www.atlantic-pub.com, 800-814-1132.

Nutritional Claims on Menus

If you decide to include menu items that are
marketed as healthy (i.e., heart healthy, low-fat,
reduced fat, cholesterol free, etc.), make sure you have
the nutritional information for these items readily
accessible. Since 1997, restaurants have been include
in the FDA's nutritional labeling laws. Any restaurant
that uses health or nutrient content claims on its men
must comply with these regulations. If you use a symb
to designate dishes as healthy, such as a heart rather
than text, you still must comply with these regulation

- **Your obligations.** Regulations state that if you
  make any nutritional claims on your menu,
  you must be able to demonstrate that there is a
  reasonable basis for making these health claims.

- **Flexibility.** Although a certain amount of flexibil
  exists regarding how restaurants set out their
  claims, they must be able to show customers an
  officials that the claim the restaurant is making
  consistent with the claims established under the
  Nutrition Labeling and Education Act.

- **Make sure you are familiar with the FDA's
  definition of terms.** While you may think a men
  item with 20 grams of fat is low-fat, the FDA may
  not define an item this way. To find out more

about the FDA regulations, you can go to their Web site at www.fda.gov.

tritional Primer

ince healthy eating represents a current food trend in the industry, it wouldn't hurt to go over a few tritional basics so that you can determine if you should clude such items on your menu. Consider the following:

- **Familiarize yourself with the six basic categories of nutrients:** proteins, fats, carbohydrates, minerals, vitamins and water. In general, for menu planning, the main categories you need to focus on are carbohydrates and fats.

- **Understand what "carbohydrates" are.** Basically, these are starches, sugars and fiber. They make up the bulk of a healthy diet and provide an important energy source. Examples of carbohydrates are sugar, potatoes, bread, rice, pasta and fruit. Vegetables also contain carbohydrates, but in much smaller amounts.

- **Fats.** Fats are a concentrated energy source and provide approximately twice as many of calories as proteins or carbohydrates. There are saturated fats and unsaturated fats. The difference relates to the fats' chemical structures. Saturated fats are more solid than unsaturated. From a health standpoint, unsaturated fats are healthier. Saturated fats include shortening and butter. Unsaturated fats include olive oil and canola oil.

- **Chronic illnesses.** Many people in the U.S. suffer from heart disease or other chronic illnesses, such as diabetes. These people are likely to constitute part of your customer base. If they make up a significant portion of your customer base, you'd be wise to familiarize yourself with various diets they have to follow. Help them adhere to their prescribe diets: include menu items that they can eat.

Communicating Nutritional Information on Your Menu

If you decide to include items on your menu that have health claims, you need to decide on the best way to communicate the nutritional information to your customer.

- **Make sure the information is correct and clear** You may want to consider hiring a dietitian to check your menu items.

- **There are software programs available that will do nutritional calculations.** ChefTec software (www.atlantic-pub.com) computes nutritional calculations. NutriBase is another nutritional software program that you can find at www.nutribase.com.

- **Nutritional information does not need to be on the menu.** You just need to make such information available. Depending on your menu format, you may not want to clutter the space with the additional information. If you find that your typical customer always requests this information however, it may be better to include it on the menu. Consider using a symbol, such as a heart, that denotes a healthy menu item. If you do this, be sure to include a definition on the menu of what the symbol means.

Provide Your Customers with Healthy, Allergy-Free Menu Alternatives

If you do not currently offer healthy menu alternatives and would like to do so, there are several options available to you:

- **Search the Web.** There are many sites that provide healthy recipes, such as the American Institute of Cancer Prevention at www.aicr.org; the American Heart Association at www.deliciousdecisions.org; and the American Diabetes Association at www. diabetes.org.

- **Books.** There are numerous good healthy cookbooks in print nowadays. The following lists but a few:
  - *Vegetarian Cooking for Everyone* by Deborah Madison
  - *The Joslin Diabetes Gourmet Cookbook* by Bonnie Sanders Polin, Ph.D. and Frances Towner Giedt
  - *The French Culinary Institute's Salute to Healthy Cooking* by Alain Sailhac, Jacques Pepin, Andre Soltner, Jacques Torres and the faculty at the French Culinary Institute
  - *Healthy Latin Cooking* by Steve Raichlen
  - *Good Food Gourmet* by Jane Brody
  - *Heart Healthy Cooking for All Seasons* by Marvin Moser, M.D., Larry Forgione, Jimmy Schmidt and Alice Waters
  - *Moosewood Restaurant Low-Fat Favorites* by the Moosewood Collective
  - *Canyon Ranch Cooking* by Jeanne Jones

- **Make less-sweeping changes.** If you don't want to spend time developing new recipes to include healthy alternatives, you could try and adapt some of your existing recipes. Try incorporating the following suggestions into your current menu program:

  - Offer at least one vegetarian entrée.

  - Offer at least one entrée without a butter or cream sauce. Try substituting a chutney or salsa for a high-calorie sauce.

  - Replace the cream or whole milk in a recipe with skim milk.

  - Replace butter on vegetables with lemon and herb.

  - Replace sour cream with yogurt.

  - Make your own stock or pick a canned stock that is low in sodium.

  - Try serving oven-baked fries rather than French fries.

  - Offer more salads.

  - Offer reduced-fat/reduced-calorie salad dressings.

  - Substitute chicken broth for milk in mashed potatoes.

  - Use olive or canola oil instead of butter or shortening.

  - Offer whole grain breads as part of a bread basket.

  - Offer low-fat mayonnaise as a sandwich condiment.

- Offer sorbet as a dessert option.

- Offer a simple fruit dessert, such as baked pears, that is low in sugar and fat.

- Offer smaller portion sizes on some of your entrées.

- Use local produce, meats and other products and let your customers know you are using them.

- **Food allergies.** A food allergy can be very serious and even life threatening. Symptoms can include hives, nausea, vomiting, shortness of breath and anaphylaxis, a severe respiratory reaction. Anyone involved in compiling menus needs to be aware of possible food allergies. Always bear in mind the following issues regarding allergies:

  - **Common allergies.** You need to know that some of the most common allergies are to nuts, eggs, shellfish, peanuts and wheat.

  - **Ingredient information.** When designing your menu, make sure ingredient information is available. If you do not list it on the menu, be certain that your servers can communicate this information accurately to your customers.

  - **Further information.** To find out more about food allergies, contact the International Food Information Council at 202-296-6540 or visit their Web site at www.ific.org.

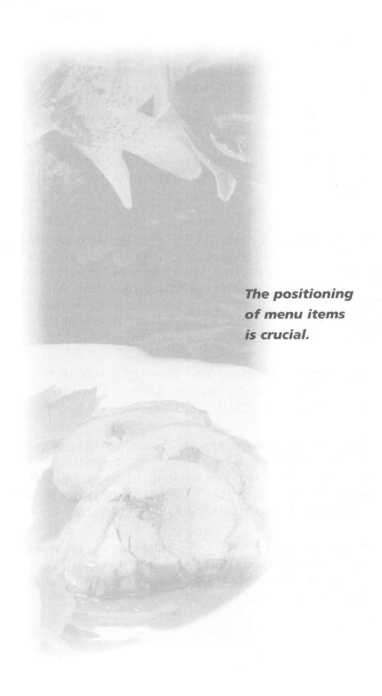

*The positioning
of menu items
is crucial.*

CHAPTER THREE

MENU DESIGN

enu Design

he goal of the menu is to direct customers to the
items that the restaurant wants to sell. The menu's
ime function should be to maximize sales and
ofits as a communication tool. There are many ways
catch customers' attention. One of these involves
e positioning of items on the menu. Generally, the
dustry uses four menu formats: single-page, two-page,
ree-page and multi-page.

Single-panel. The focal point on a single-page menu
is the area in the top half of the page. Use this area
of the menu to promote your most profitable items.

FOCAL POINT
promote your most
profitable items here

- **Two-panel.** On a two-panel menu, customers first
  focus on the left-hand side of the open menu - just
  like reading a book - then continue across the top
  of the page, to the right, and then down the right-
  hand side. Make the most of the left-hand side.

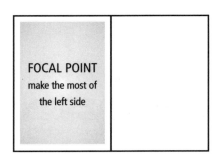

- **Three-panel.** The three-panel menu gives you a total of six spaces to use for menu copy. With these menus, the eye focuses in the center. Position items you want to sell most on the insid center page.

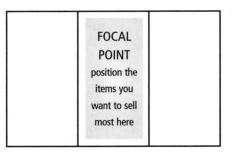

- **Multi-page.** It is harder to locate the focal point a multi-page menu. Each page spread becomes i own "mini-menu," with focal points similar to tw panel menus. Make the most of each mini focal point.

nu Size and Cover

s with the menu content, the menu cover should reflect your restaurant's individual identity. member, the cover is the first place on paper where ı can communicate your identity to the customer. In ıeral, restaurants use menu covers or holders that : 9 inches wide by 12-inches tall. This size easily ıds an 8-1/2- by 11-inch sheet of paper. Of course, ıer sizes can work as well. Menu size is determined, gely, by the number of items on the menu. When ı igning your menu cover, bear in mind the following:

- **Manageability.** Keep in mind that the menu size should be manageable for the customers. Remember that they are often maneuvering in a limited space that includes water, wineglasses, candles, table tents and flowers.

- **Logos, graphics and text.** Include graphics (the establishment's logo) and text. If your restaurant is in an historic building, for instance, you may want to include a drawing or photo of the building on your cover. If you are operating a family restaurant that has been in existence for generations, you may want to put a paragraph or two of copy with your family's food philosophy or the family history.

- **Construction.** The cover material should be made from durable material; its main function is to protect interior pages. Consider leather, vinyl, laminated paper or plastic sleeves. Your establishment's identity will help you choose the appropriate cover material. A fine-dining restaurant would not use plastic sleeves. But, for a mid-price family restaurant, plastic sleeve menu covers would be appropriate.

- **Color.** The cover color should also be chosen wit[h] care. The color should tie into the theme and dé[cor] of your restaurant. Remember, however, that co[lor] has psychological impact. Choose colors that ev[oke] pleasant images. From a financial standpoint, bear in mind that the more colors you use for y[our] menu, the more expensive the printing process becomes.

- **General information.** You may also want to include general information on the cover, such as your hours of operation, address, telephone number, credit cards that you accept and any special services that you provide. While your regular customers may not need this informatio[n] new customers will appreciate it.

Menu Text

Menu text can influence what your customers choose to purchase. Menu copy should clearly communicate what the customer will receive so there are no surprises. Let the copy reflect your restaurant' identity. Here are some suggestions for enhancing the content of your menu:

- **Don't make false claims.** Diners are becoming more and more sophisticated. For example, if you claim the mashed potatoes are homemade, your customer is likely to know. If you make fal[se] claims, customers will feel aggrieved. You will lo[se] customers along with potential profits.

- **Quality copy.** Make sure that you:
  - Use short phrases in your descriptions.

  - Don't overuse adjectives.

- Use descriptive, food-associated words (e.g., say "roasted" rather than "cooked").

- **Avoid over-description.** It can make the dish seem like a confusing mess of ingredients rather than a deliciously enticing meal. For example, if you were a restaurant customer, which of the following descriptions would be more likely to influence you? While both descriptions convey the same information, the first one actually has the opposite of the desired effect. The first one almost makes you feel too full from just reading the description; the second description is more likely to make you crave the item:

Veal Parmigiana – tender veal lightly breaded and fried to perfection, then smothered with thick marinara sauce and topped with layers of melted provolone cheese, served with a mound of linguini.

Veal Parmigiana – lightly breaded and fried veal topped with marinara sauce and provolone cheese. Served with a side of linguini.

---

nu Copy

Menu copy can be divided into three general categories: name of the item, descriptive copy and eral copy. The most important and trickiest of these egories is the description. Some restaurants have g, detailed descriptions, while others are very brief. w do you determine what is right for your establish- nt? What kind of food do you serve? Are ingredients nmon to most households or do you offer a variety xotic foods? Is a meal at your restaurant paced slow ast? Remember, longer descriptions will slow down order-taking process. Consider the following when ating copy for your menu:

- **Menu copy should include the following basic information:**

  - Preparation method (grilled, sautéed, fried, et
  - Main ingredients.
  - How it is served/accompaniments.
  - Grades and/or freshness claims.
  - Geographic origin (Copper River salmon, Dov sole, etc.).

- **Names.** Clearly define the item. Some items, such as hamburger or roasted chicken, are easy to name. Others are less obvious: Lisa's Favorite Salad, Mountain Burger or Theater Steak, for example. Expand the description for such items.

- **Descriptive copy.** This includes ingredients, method of preparation and any side dishes that accompany the entrée. There's no need to embellish every item with descriptive copy. If something is grilled, you really don't need to say any more about it. If, however, you're serving a dish such as foie gras in a mid-price family restaurant, you'll probably want to include a few descriptive phrases!

- **General copy.** Information about the estab- lishment (e.g., hours of operation, location and ownership) should be kept simple.

- **Foreign words.** Use them, by all means - but be careful. If it isn't self-explanatory, explain the phrase. Your customers are unlikely to order something they can't understand.

ce Placement

osition prices on the menu so as to ensure that the
customer reads the description before reading the price.

• Rather than using dot leaders and placing prices
  in a row along the right-hand side of the page
  (Example 1), try placing the prices right after the
  last word of the item's description (Example 2).
  This will help shift the focus away from the prices.

Example 1

> **Shrimp Lo Mein** – Shrimp, vegetables,
> scallions and egg noodles.............................$7.95
>
> **Cashew Chicken** – Crispy chicken, ginger brown
> sauce, roasted cashews and vegetables $6.95
>
> **Pepper Steak** – Onion, ginger peppercorn beef
> and vegetables...$8.95

Example 2

> **Shrimp Lo Mein** – Shrimp, vegetables,
> scallions and egg noodles $7.95
>
> **Cashew Chicken** – Crispy chicken, ginger brown
> sauce, roasted cashews and vegetables $6.95
>
> **Pepper Steak** – Onion, ginger peppercorn beef
> and vegetables $8.95

Avoid printing prices in bold. Also, never over-
write price increases so that the diner can see the
previous, lower price.

Arrangement of Text

Just as important as price placement is how the te
is arranged on the menu. Menus tend to be arran;
logically, in the order in which the courses are served
appetizers, soups and salads come before entrées.
Desserts are the final menu item. While eye flow of th
menu is important, the customer must still be able to
easily locate the type of food that he or she wants. Be
guided by the following:

- **Item placement.** Restaurant consultants tend t
  agree that item placement is extremely importar
  It affects product sales. Customers are most like
  to remember the first and last things they read
  hear. By placing the items you want to sell (the
  items that yield the highest profits) first or last,
  you increase the chance of selling them. Look at
  the following example menu quickly, then look
  away. Which items do you recall?

ENTRÉES

Baked Trout with White Wine Herb Sauce $18.95

New York Strip with Roasted Potatoes $19.95

Double Cut Maple Glazed Pork Chops with
Whipped Sweet Potatoes $16.95

Beef Tenderloin Kabob over Wild Rice Pilaf $20.75

Roast Chicken with Cornbread Sage Stuffing $15.75

Eggplant Napoleon with Goat Cheese $14.75

- **Maximize position.** You probably recalled the trout, the strip steak, the napoleon and the chicken from the previous example. Place the items you want sell most in a similar position. You want to sell the trout and steak because they will increase your check averages and your profits. The chicken and the vegetarian option will have low food costs, so selling those will also help your profit margin.

- **Lower-profit items.** Draw attention away from low-profit items by placing them in the middle of the list.

nu Psychology

well-designed menu influences what customers choose to buy. Everything from the type to the r to the item placement has an effect on what your tomer may purchase. As with any advertising, you direct your customer's attention to particular areas items and influence their purchasing decisions.

- **Left to right.** Remember that in western culture, people's eye movement goes from left to right and starts at the top of the page. Different menu formats will require different item placement because of the way the human eye moves across the page.

- **Eye movement can also be influenced by a "magnet."** Any kind of box or graphic image will make the reader move his or her eye away from the normal pattern to this area. Place items you want to sell in these areas - you're more likely to sell them.

- **Your menu is your vehicle for telling your customers what your restaurant is about.** If y restaurant is about fast food at a low price, let your menu say this! Design your menu to reflect these values. If speed is one part of your identity think about how you can reflect this in your me What colors and graphic elements denote speed? Perhaps some of the menu items could have graphic elements that look like the trails the Roa Runner left in old cartoons. Red is often a color used for sports cars, so you may want to use red and other bright colors for your menu.

Layout and Graphics

Work closely with your printer and/or designer on typeface styles and sizes. You want a typeface th echoes the theme or style of your restaurant. Above a make sure the type is readable.

- **Spacing.** How the text looks is important. Be su to have enough white space on the menu. A mer that is cluttered is very hard to read and annoyi to customers. If you do have a large area of blan space on your menu, use this to advertise daily specials or drink or dessert specialties.

- **Typefaces.** Your printer has access to catalogs and can explain some of the nuances of choosin typefaces, but here are some basics: Typefaces appropriate for menus are serif (**PRIME RIB**), sa serif (**PRIME RIB**) and script (*Prime Rib*).Serif has tiny lines at the end of letters and looks traditio or old-fashioned. Sans serif type is simpler and has a blocky shape, it looks more modern. Scrip should be used sparingly because the slant of th letters can create eyestrain for the reader.

- **Design.** Here are a few more design suggestions:

  - **Print the copy using both uppercase and lowercase letters,** using the upper case for food categories or to draw attention to a special or original item. Use lowercase letters for item descriptions.

  - **Use bold or italic type to break up large blocks of text.** For example, you can put your menu groups in bold, the menu item names in italic and the descriptive copy in regular type.

  - **Don't use more than three type styles on your menu.** This can create a confusing and haphazard appearance.

  - **Select type size that fits the space you have,** but, in general, type should be no ..... smaller than 12 points (type size is measured in points).

  - **Spacing between letters is adjustable.** This is called kerning. Kerning can be adjusted to make your text more readable.

  - **The spacing between lines of text is called leading.** It is adjustable as well. Leading should be at least 3 points between lines for maximum readability.

  - **Graphic elements.** If you decide to incorporate graphic elements into your menu, you can easily add simple geometric designs using a word-processing program. If you want pictures, however, there are several options.

  - **If you have a photograph, work with your printer to incorporate this.**

- **You can download free clip art** from online sources, including www.clip-art.com, www.barrysclipart.com and www.clipartconnection.com.

- **If you want an original illustration, check around area colleges.** You can probably find a student artist at a reasonable price.

Menu Production

The quality of the material you use to produce the menu will be determined largely by how frequently you decide to reprint your menu. Bear in mind the following:

- **Frequency of reprints.** If the menu changes oft« you may want to choose lower-quality, lower-priced paper stock. If your menu isn't likely to change often, you may want to go with the highe quality, or laminate your menu for increased durability. Laminate is an excellent idea because it also helps keep your menus clean. Nothing detracts from a person's appetite quicker than being handed a dirty, stained menu.

- **Other production considerations.** Factors you will need to consider when you go to print with your menu are paper type and weight, color and ink.

- **Cover material.** For the cover, consider a heavie paper stock, such as "cover stock." It works well for restaurant menus. Regular letter paper cann« stand up to constant handling as well as heavier stock.

- **Paper color.** Finally, you need to decide the color of your menu paper. Be sure that your color choice echoes your décor and the restaurant's identity as a whole. If you're known as a cozy, romantic dinner bistro, don't choose bright, glaring colors for your menu. Use subtle shades that reflect your restaurant's personality.

- **Laser paper.** Many office supply stores offer laser printer papers that you can use for your menu and menu cover. You can also order papers online at www.ideaart.com.

nu Design Dos and Don'ts

Vork on your menu layout yourself; don't leave it to the printer. The printer can balance the menu d make it aesthetically pleasing, but you know which ms you want to emphasize. If you feel unsure about w to approach this, hire a menu consultant. Also, put me thought into the following:

- **Leave some eye "breathing" room.** A menu with too much text will overwhelm your customers.

- **Make sure the type size is large enough to read.** This is really important if your tables are lit with candlelight. You may want to try reading your copy under the same conditions before you send it off to the printer. Don't go below 12-point type. Make sure that the type is readable as well.

- **Prices.** Don't print all your prices in a row down the right-hand side of the page. This will draw your customer's attention to the price rather than the product.

- **Don't waste space describing common items.** Pause to consider how much (or how little) descriptive text you want on your menu.

- **Proofread.** Be sure to proofread, and have someone else proofread, your menu before sendi: it off to the printer. There is nothing more unpro fessional than a menu with typos! International Menu Speller (www.atlantic-pub.com) is a dictionary computer program that contains nam< of thousands of food items and can be loaded rig into your computer.

Sample Menus

The next page contains a fictitious example of a mer for an upper-price, urban restaurant:

- **Explanations.** The following simple, one-page menu has short descriptive copy for items that probably need some form of explanation. Salads are self-explanatory; desserts are not elaborated upon because the manager relies on servers to g customers this information.

- **Simplicity.** To keep the clean, elegant look that echoed in the restaurant's décor, the menu does not incorporate graphic elements. Nor does it try to crowd the menu with too much information. A separate wine and beer list is used. The colors would also be simple - perhaps a beige paper an< black ink.

- **Avoid confusion.** There is some variety in the fonts (script, bold, italic and regular) and point sizes (14 and 12) used, but not enough to make things look confusing.

- **Prices.** Place prices after the last descriptive phrase so the customer will not focus on them. Also, position the items with the highest profitability first and last on the menu.

To Start

Cedar Planked Salmon Salad $4.95
Salmon grilled on a cedar plank, served with an herbed couscous lentil salad

Blue Cheese Baklava $3.75
Layers of phyllo, Maytag blue cheese and honeyed almonds

Lobster Spring Rolls with Basil Oil $5.25
esh lobster with spring mix and basil oil, served cold with a chili oil dipping sauce

Entrées

Seared Tuna with Black Pepper Crust $22.95
Served with braised bok choy and wasabi mashed potatoes

Filet mignon with Gorgonzola Butter Sauce $18.95
6-oz portion grilled to your taste and served with fresh roasted asparagus and sweet potato latkes

Orecchiette with Garlic Cream Sauce $13.95
Served with haricot vert and Italian bread

Maple Glazed Pork Chops $16.95
Two 6-oz pork chops glazed with a maple soy sauce and served with whipped sweet potatoes and roasted apple rings

Dessert

Chocolate Espresso Crème Brûlée $7.00
Raspberry Mocha Torte $8.75

The menu on the following page is for a fictitious lunch diner. Consider the following:

- **Homey ambiance.** The name of the restaurant and the graphic elements give the customer a sense of a homey establishment that will offer "comfort" food at reasonable prices.

- **Prices.** While this menu does put the prices in more of a line, the prices themselves are so similar in each category that it will probably have little effect on the customers' choices.

- **Extra description.** This icon is provided for the items that "Nancy recommends." It has the effect of steering the customer in the right direction.

- **Fonts.** The size of text on the menu is at least 12 point, and three different fonts are used to vary the text and make it easy for the customer to differentiate between categories and text.

- **Color.** For this menu, the owner/manager would probably use colored paper - maybe a bright green or yellow. It could be a single- or double-page menu, and it would probably be inside a plastic menu cover or laminated.

......NANCY'S DINER......

......SALADS......

Chicken Salad Plate with grapes, greens & crackers   4.95

Tuna Salad Plate with grapes, greens & crackers   4.95

Tossed Salad with choice of dressing   1.75

Trio Salad with cottage cheese, chicken salad & fruit   5.95

......BURGERS......

Mountain – a half pound of ground sirloin with all the trimmings   6.95

Veggie Patch – a quarter-pound ground sirloin with tomato, lettuce & onion   5.95

Cheese Lover's – a quarter-pound ground sirloin with cheddar, Monterey jack & Swiss   6.25

Mexican – a quarter-pound ground sirloin with cheddar cheese, salsa & avocado   6.25

......BEVERAGES......

Sodas   1.50
Coffee   1.25
Iced Tea   1.50

......SIDES......

French Fries   .95
Mashed Potatoes   1.50
Onion Rings   1.25

......SOUPS......

Soup du jour
cup 1.25   bowl 2.50

Beef Vegetable
cup 1.25   bowl 2.50

❀**Ben's White Lightening Chili**
Made with chicken, white beans & green chilis
cup 2.25   bowl 3.50

......SANDWICHES......

Grilled Chicken on a sesame bun with Swiss cheese, lettuce & tomato   6.95

Meatloaf – served on thick, crusty bread with a side of ketchup   6.50

Steak & Cheese – served on a hoagie bun with choice of mushroom or tomato sauce   6.95

❀**Egg Salad** – Nancy's own recipe. Served on white or wheat bread with a pickle   5.75

Veggie – tomato, cucumber, sprouts, avocado & melted Swiss or cheddar cheese on your choice of bread   4.95

......DESSERTS......

Brownie Cake   3.95

❀**Nancy's Homemade Apple Pie**   3.50

Blueberry Pie   3.25

❀ Nancy's Favorites

Promote items such as desserts and appetizers.

CHAPTER FOUR

MENU MANAGEMENT SUPPORTS

ce and Profit

efore you can put a menu-pricing system into
place, you must develop systems that will help you
cument your procedures so you can make decisions
t will lead to greater profits and increased revenues.
t perhaps you should take a step back. First, ask
irself, what kind of profits do I need to realize for this
be a viable business?

- **Food - Itemize ingredient costs.** When you are
  trying to determine what to charge for menu items,
  one of the first things you look at is food cost.

- **Figure out your total costs per month.** These
  costs include overhead, labor and food. Say you
  serve 200 entrées per day. Your daily costs to
  operate are $2400, and your profit goal is 10
  percent of sales. In order to cover your costs and
  realize your target profit, your menu entrées need to
  sell for $12.

- **Profitability.** Obviously, everything on your menu
  won't cost $12, but you should try to emphasize
  the items that are $12 or more. This will help
  influence your customers to buy these items and
  keep your check averages up.

- **Promote.** Introduce a separate dessert menu or a
  dessert cart to take to customers for viewing.

- **Influence the customer.** If the entrées you are
  selling are low value, you'll have to try to make ι
  the difference by selling appetizers, sides, drinks
  and desserts. If you have to do this to get your
  check average up, remember to have your server
  use suggestive selling techniques.

Menu Sales Analysis

Menu sales analysis, or menu scores, track how
many of each menu item is sold. Looking at this
information, together with food cost and menu prices,
can give the food service manager a great deal of
information. Look at the following:

- **Sales mix.** Study the menu sales mix. Determin
  which menu items should be emphasized. Often
  when profits aren't as good as the manager wan'
  labor, waste, over-portioning or rising food cost ι
  blamed. Managers should also consider the men
  as the potential problem.

- **Emphasize the mix of items and keep your
  food costs under control.** Concentrating on the
  mix is one of the best ways to realize the highest
  profit possible. Rather than focusing on the prof
  of individual menu items, you should concentra'
  on what kind of profit you are achieving from yo
  menu as a whole.

- **Avoid negatively impacting your check
  average.** In an attempt to contain food costs, do
  emphasize only low-cost items. Usually items th
  have a low food cost also have a low menu price
  (items such as chicken and vegetarian meals). If
  your customers are predominantly buying thes

items, your check average will be too low to realize the profit you desire. If, on the other hand, you are only emphasizing high-cost, high-price items like steak and seafood, you are probably increasing your food cost so much that it is eating into profits.

lysis Simplified

Ianagers have different ways of analyzing their sales mix. This may range from simply looking a cash register report at the end of each night, to ing an intuitive feeling for which items are selling, to ating a complicated way of categorizing each menu n in order to analyze the sales mix. Some of these thods focus on controlling food costs to increase prof-ility and others focus on increasing sales of more fitable items. While the more complicated methods e their advantages, most food service managers are d pressed for time, and more than likely they can't eeze even one more hour out of their week to analyze nu sales. The following guidelines represent a "middle und." You can still get the information you need from ales analysis, but you don't have to devote a great l of time to computation:

- **When you're looking at your menu sales mix, you are interested in three things:**
    1. How many of an item are sold

    2. Item cost

    3. Item profitability

- **Computerized reports.** Make life easy. Consider installing a computerized cash register. It only takes seconds to print off a report on what items sold nightly, weekly and monthly.

- **Manual system.** If your restaurant doesn't have a computerized register, you can track a period of time - let's say a month - and get this information by pulling it off guest checks. This may be an ideal duty to add to your cashiers' or servers' job description. Have them transpose this information a tracking sheet for you. Costs can easily be pulle from your standardized recipes or cost sheets.

Making the Figures Work for You

Now that you have this information, you can see which menu items are popular, which are high-cost, low-cost, high-profit and low-profit. Pull all this information into a simple table so you can compare it easily. A menu item's profit margin refers to what the item contributes to the overall profit of a restaurant. The amount an item contributes is the difference between the menu price and the item's food cost. To determine this you will need to look at monthly financ statements. Pull your total food costs off this, then subtract it from your total sales. The following is a practical example of how to set out your figure:

ITEM	POPULARITY*	COST	MENU	PROFIT MARGIN
Hamburger Plate	36/100	$0.62	$5.50	$4.88
Spaghetti Carbonara	15/100	$1.79	$6.25	$4.46
Seafood Combo Plate	49/100	$3.40	$10.95	$7.55
*36/100 means 36 hamburger plates were sold out of a total of 100 entrées served in that time period.				

- **Now what do you do with this information on you have it?** What does this information tell yo about how you can increase profits? Look at you table. You'll see that your hamburger plate was almost as popular as your seafood plate. But the hamburger plate costs you a good deal less. You can increase profits by focusing on such lower-cost items.

- **Increase your profit margin by decreasing your food costs.** While on the surface this is true, keep in mind that your guest checks' sales will also be lower. For example, on the night you sold 100 entrées, you paid out $22.32 for the hamburger plates; the profit margin was $175.68. With your seafood plate, however, you spent $166.60; your profit margin was $369.95. So, even though your food-cost percentage was higher, you doubled your profit margin with the seafood plate.

- **Focus on menu items that have a high profit-ability,** whether these items have high or low food costs. But remember, you must decide what works best for you and your establishment. Whatever strategy you choose to follow, the information itself will help you make menu design decisions that will increase your profitability.

:iding Which Items to Promote

[aving worked your costs, the next step is to decide which menu items you want to focus on and v you should place them on your menu. The items t are high-profit or low-cost should be featured minently. Items that you are trying to downplay, due iigh-cost or low-profitability, should be "hidden" in ir menu. Consider the following:

- **Promotions.** If you are trying to increase an item's popularity, place the item in a visible spot so the customer is more likely to order it.

Suggestions on how to increase item profitability:

- **You can increase prices on your better-selling items** and see if it affects your sales. If your sal don't drop because of the increase you will see a greater profit.

- **Have your servers focus on suggestive selling techniques** to promote the items where you wan to increase sales.

- **Decrease the portion size on some of your higher-cost items** to decrease food cost.

- **If you have a low-cost item that isn't selling well, add an inexpensive side item** and see if this boosts sales.

Sales History

Many of your managerial duties involve paperwork and without accurate paperwork it is difficult to forecast your sales, purchase appropriate amounts of inventory and schedule needed labor. The bottom line is that you need to price your menu so you will see a profit.

- **Develop a sales history.** Basically, this details your previous sales records. The record should be kept as a daily log and should include the following information:
  - Customer Counts

  - Daily Sales

  - Daily Costs

• **Additional information.** You may find it useful to record other information as well. Things you might want to record include: weather, special events in the area and any internal operational changes. For example, if you experienced an extremely slow Saturday night last year, you could look back and see that on that particular Saturday there was a heavy snowstorm. You could also track whether or not the live music you added on Thursday nights was impacting your sales.

• **Make the sales history as easy, or as complicated, as you want.** The more information you track, the more information you have at your disposal to help with decision making. Here's a simplified example of a sales history:

E 1/15/03			
AGNA #/$	**RAVIOLI #/$**	**DAILY SALES**	**DAILY COSTS**
$111.30	22/$152.90	$649.50	$362.90

OF CUSTOMERS: 97
JSTOMER NOTES: *Training a new cook*

• **Look at the above example.** Compare a given date to the same date last year. You may find that last year's costs were much lower. By looking at the note column in the sales history, the manager can see that on this particular date the restaurant may have been running at a higher cost because of the training.

• **Extra useful information.** Compare the number of lasagna sales from last year to this year. This comparison will tell you many things. If sales are down from last year, it may be time to revamp the dish. Perhaps you should make it a specialty

item by changing the ingredients or adding items
The manager may also want to consider the item
menu placement. Perhaps, by your featuring
lasagna more prominently on the menu, sales wi
pick up. On the other hand, it may be time to dr
the item from the menu. The manager can analy
current food trends to help make this decision.

- **Computerized registers.** Point-of-sale systems
  (POS) can do most of this work for you. For a
  comparison of many of the electronic systems
  available, go to www.cookeryonline.com/Link%2(
  Frames/POS.html.

The Production Sheet

The production sheet is a device used to establish
production controls. It records an estimate of how
many servings of each menu item will be sold and
how many need to be prepared for a particular service
period. Here's an example of a production sheet:

DATE: 5/14/03
SERVICE PERIOD: Dinner
CHEF/MANAGER: J. Schmidt

ITEM	# TO PREP	PORTION COST	FOOD COST	# SERVED	ACTL COS
Rib Eye Steak	25	$4.25	$106.25	20	$85.0
Pasta Primavera	16	$2.10	$33.60	22	$46.2

- **Update the production sheet daily.** After the
  service period, record the actual number of each
  item sold, along with actual food cost.

- **Estimating made easy.** Together with the day's sales history, these figures will help you estimate future sales with greater accuracy. It will also provide you with information on which to base future decisions.

- **Accountability.** The production sheet shows you how well your menu prices are accounting for food costs. If your food costs are consistently higher than the costs you used to calculate prices, consider raising your menu prices.

od-Cost Tracking

ost is the basic building block of menu pricing, so you need to understand food cost in order to price ur menu for maximum profits. Before you price your enu, you need to cost out each item. This information n come from your standardized recipe, or you can eate a separate cost sheet that lists all the items on e menu. Then figure out the cost for each of these.

- **Costs should be based on a standardized recipe.** Bear in mind, however, that while the standardized recipe is an obvious place to list menu item costs, it may not be the best place. More than likely you and your kitchen staff aren't keeping current with cost changes. So, if the only place that cost is listed is the recipe, try keeping menu item cost information on a separate sheet with your invoices and other purchasing paperwork. This way you can easily monitor your food costs and keep track of any changes.

- **Update your menu item costs at least once a month.** Remember, prices, particularly fresh produce prices, can fluctuate wildly.

- **Compare menu prices to menu item costs on a regular basis.** This way you will know when you need to change menu prices to reflect increased food costs (the cost of food, like most things, has a tendency to increase over time). If you monitor your cost and prices, you will be able to change prices before your profits begin to spiral downwards.

Here's an example of a tally sheet you can use to keep track of costs:

ITEM	DATE	COST	MENU PRICE
Fish & Chips Dinner	2/03	$1.09	$6.75
	3/03	$1.07	
	4/03	$1.24	
Meatloaf Dinner	2/03	$2.20	$7.25
	3/03	$2.20	
	4/03	$2.24	

Figuring Food Cost

Armed with cost information, you are now in a position to establish your menu prices. Remember, however, that prices will also have to take indirect factors into consideration.

- **Calculate food costs.** Usually, food cost is expressed as a percentage of the menu price or of overall sales. Food cost of a specific menu item is figured by dividing the cost of the ingredients for the item by the menu price. This figure is expressed as a percentage. For example: $3.80 (ingredient food cost) ÷ $12.50 (selling price) = .30 (30% food cost).

- **Record overall food costs on a monthly income statement.** These numbers will help you decide how well your restaurant operation is doing.

- **Use your monthly figures.** High monthly food costs can be an indication of many things: the need for employee training, the need to adjust menu prices to reflect costs better, overpurchasing, waste and theft, to name but a few.

- **Set targets.** Define realistic food-cost targets for your establishment.

- **Determine the revenue you can make from an item.** Look at the cost, the menu price and your sales history. If you divide the total income into the total cost of the item, you can determine food cost for a particular period of time. For example, say you sold 200 items during a month: $760 (cost of $3.80 multiplied by 200) ÷ $2,500 (sold 200 at $12.50) = 30% food cost.

- **Use your sales history to forecast which items will sell in the future.** It can help you evaluate how much to purchase and prepare. It can even help you reduce kitchen labor costs.

- **Poor menu design?** If you're not reaching your food cost goals or are not achieving as high a profit margin as you would like, it may be because of your menu design. Are you emphasizing high-food-cost or low-profit items? Change the design of your menu. It will help decrease food cost and increase profits. Remember, if you sell too many high-cost items, your food cost will go up, because many of these (such as beef and seafood) have a high cost. On the other hand, if you sell too many low-cost items, your check averages and gross profits will decline. When designing your menu, you will want to have a mix of both these types of items.

- **Keep in mind that there's a difference between actual food cost and target food cost.** Every restaurant has a food-cost percentage or a food-cost-percentage range that they strive to obtain. Often, managerial bonuses are tied to reaching such food-cost goals.

- **Moving targets.** It's a month-to-month battle to keep your ever-changing food costs in your target area. Just remember, your actual food cost is what you actually spend on ingredients. While your target food costs may be 32 percent, last March your actual food costs might have been 38 percent. Identify the reasons for this difference - it's an important factor in controlling food costs.

Lowering Food Cost

One way to increase your profits is by lowering your food cost. There are several ways to do this:

- **Work with your kitchen staff** on this one. One of the major culprits in high food costs is waste. Put a new garbage can in the kitchen. This can is for wasted product only, such as wrong orders, dropped food, etc. By giving your kitchen staff this visual aid, you can reinforce the amount of money that gets spent on such product waste. This will help keep your staff tuned in to keeping on eye on kitchen waste.

- **Pick a month to have the entire staff work to lower food cost.** If you're running a 38 percent food cost, tell your employees you want to try to lower it to 36 percent that month. Give them an incentive; throw a party at the end of the month if the goal is achieved. Create T-shirts and prizes to give away at the party. For example, offer a prize for the server who sold the most desserts that month or the cook who came up with the best new cost-saving measure. Not only will you cut your costs, but you'll also build employee morale and loyalty at the same time.

• **Make sure your cooks are using scales and measuring ingredients.** Often cooks will "free-hand it" after a while. Set up a scale. After the cook prepares an item the usual way, have the same cook prepare the item using a scale and/or measuring devices. Show the staff the difference in ingredient amounts.

• **Make sure you shop for purveyors.** Don't rest once you've found one. "Comparison" shop on a continual basis.

• **Look at vendors' product labels for box strength.** This will tell you where the product came from. Most manufacturers won't ship more than 100 miles away from their plants. The further away that a supplier is located, the more shipping will cost.

• **Consider using local producers.** You can also use this as a promotional device. If you use local produce, let your customers know!

- **Substitute premade items** for some items you used to make from scratch. You don't have to sacrifice quality. Many premade items are good. You can also start with a premade item and add ingredients. For instance, you can buy a premade salad dressing and add blue cheese or fresh herb Use these items to lower your food and labor cost you can still put out a quality item.

Yield Tests

A yield test is used to determine the amount of a product that is edible and the amount that is wast Inventory yield tests should be carried out on a regular basis, especially on items that have a high perishabilit rate. Don't waste money on items that yield little edibl product! Consider the following:

- **Quality.** Higher-quality items will usually provide more edible product, so it's really important to be able to recognize high-quality products. Factors to look out for when deciding on product quality include:
  - Weight
  - Texture
  - Grade
  - Odor
  - Packaging
  - Temperature
  - Color
  - Size

- **Two types of yield tests.** There are two yield tests: a convenience yield test and a fresh-food yield test. Convenience yield tests are conducted on prepackaged products and generally consist o taking the item out of its packaging and weighing it. Fresh-food yield tests are more complicated and should involve the following steps:

- Weigh the product when it is received and again when it comes out of storage.

- Trim excess fat, bones, etc., and weigh.

- Wash and weigh the item again.

- Prepare the food and weigh again to determine the amount of weight lost during the cooking process.

- Cut the item into portion sizes.

- Weigh the portions.

- **Record each stage of the yield test.** This information will help you decide whether or not you are wasting money on a high percentage of unusable product.

andardized Recipes

The standardized recipe is an important tool for the food service manager. Use of a standardized recipe sures quality and consistency of menu items. It also lps with cost control and menu pricing.

re are some of the advantages of using standardized recipes:

- Ensures product consistency.
- Improves cost control by controlling portion size.
- Lists item cost, which makes it easy to access and use this information for pricing.
- Helps make the kitchen run smoother and more efficiently.

- Helps create inventory and purchasing lists.
- Helps with employee training.

Consider the following when developing your recipe file:

- **Test all recipes in your kitchen.** Your kitchen's oven may cook muffins quicker than the oven us to create the recipe. If you don't test and find thi out, your cooks will constantly burn the muffins because they are using the wrong cooking time.

- **Have ingredients listed in the order in which they are used.**

- **Check for correct ingredient amounts.**

- **Make sure the sequence of activities is clear.**

- **Make sure you have all the necessary equipment** to prepare the recipe. If your staff is using various pans to cook something because you don't have the correct size, the item will not turn out the same each time and you will forfeit consistency.

- **Measure dry ingredients by weight and liquid ingredients by volume.** Be sure you have a scal to measure the weighed amounts.

- **Make sure that you or a designated person records any changes** to the recipe over time.

- **Use it!** Make sure you enforce the use of standa ized recipes with your kitchen staff.

- **Recipe holders.** Use index cards and an index-card holder to hold your recipes. Alternatively, u

a three-ring binder with recipe sheets inserted into
transparent envelopes that can be easily wiped
clean.

• **Organize your file in a meaningful way.** Group
all the appetizers together, all the soups, all the
entrées, all the salads and all the desserts.

ipe Information

lthough your recipe file will change over time,
it should always contain certain basic pieces of
ormation. Make sure that you keep track of these
nges and keep your file up to date. The following
summary of the essential information you need to
lude on your recipe form:

• **Name of item.**

• **Recipe number**/identification within file system.

• **Yield.** Record the total quantity that the recipe will
yield.

• **Portion size.** List portions by weight or number
of pieces. You may want to include what size of
utensil to use for serving; for example, the 6-oz
ladle for a cup of soup.

• **Garnishes.** Be specific and make sure every plate
goes out looking the same. This includes plate
setup. You may want to draw a diagram or include
a photograph to show your staff how the chicken
should lean up against the polenta squares and
how the asparagus should sit at an angle on the
other side of the chicken.

- **Ingredients.** List ingredients in order. Make sur to list quantities of ingredients used, and keep t abbreviation used for quantities consistent. If yo use "oz" for ounce in one recipe, make sure you use it in all your recipes. Give the physical state of ingredients – are the nuts whole or chopped? the flour sifted?

- **Preparation instructions.** Be sure to include a preheating instructions. Use the correct terms for instructions. Do you want the eggs mixed in the batter or folded into it? Should the employe stir or mix with an electric mixer? Be sure to include any precautions or special instructions. When preparing caramel, for example, caution the preparers that the sugar water is extremely hot and that they should take the mixture off th heat before adding the cream. These instruction should also include pan sizes and preparation times, cooking temperatures, cooking times, how to test for doneness and instructions for portioning.

- **Finishing.** Describe any finish that the product needs, such as a brushing of oil or melted chocolate drizzled on top. Also, include how to cool and at what temperature the product shou be held. Can it sit at room temperature or does need to be refrigerated?

- **Cost.** Not all restaurants include cost on the reci If you do, the recipe can be used as a resource fo everyday ordering, as well as menu design. Includ every ingredient and every garnish for accuracy. You will need to look at product invoices to get un prices, then determine the ingredient cost from th Total the cost of each ingredient for your total rec cost. Divide by the number of portions. This will g you the portion cost.

e a look at the following example of a recipe card:

ipe No. 126	Name: Blue Ridge Jambalaya
ion size: 1.5 cups	Yields: 40 portions
t Per Portion: $0.90	

redients	Weight/Measure	Cost
:ken, boneless breast cut in 1-inch pieces	4 lbs	$8.00
ouille sausage, sliced	2 lbs	$5.58
ry, chopped	16 cups	$3.16
peppers, chopped	8 each	$6.00
ɔns, chopped	4 each	$0.40
ic cloves, minced	8 each	$0.17
rt-grain brown rice, dry	6 cups	$4.74
r	32 oz	$3.50
:ken stock	60 oz	$1.72
ned diced tomato	60 oz	$2.12
ısco sauce	4 tsp	$0.03
ley (garnish)		$0.04
ıbread (side)		$0.58
		$36.04

:ctions:

chicken and cut into 1-inch pieces. Heat vegetable oil in a large sauté
. Add chicken and cook through. Add sausage and heat through. In
ge stockpot, sauté onion, garlic, celery and red pepper in oil. Add
and coat rice with oil. Turn heat down to low, add beer and broth a
at a time, allowing the rice to absorb the liquid before adding more.
n rice has simmered about 15-20 minutes, add tomato, chicken and
age. Continue cooking until done and rice is tender (about 1 hour).
Tabasco, salt and pepper. Portion out the jambalaya into smaller
:ainers to cool. Can refrigerate or use immediately for service.

vice: Serve in a dinner bowl with a piece of cornbread on the side.
with parsley.

Pricing is a major component of your menu.

CHAPTER FIVE

MENU PRICING

eral Considerations

bviously, menu pricing is a major component of menu management. When you put a price on menu 1s, your overall goal is to realize a profit. Pricing may n like a mathematical exercise or a lucky guess, but neither of these. Pricing is based on a markup of t, which is figured by determining food cost, sales ory and profit margin. But pricing strategy does not there. Consider the following:

- **Pricing decisions.** They are influenced by indirect factors, such as:
  - Human psychology
  - Market conditions
  - Location
  - Atmosphere
  - Service style
  - Competition
  - Customers' willingness to pay

- **Never forget that prices are demand or market driven.** When the economy is bad, restaurants are likely to see reduced profits because people may be eating out and traveling less. The market will

ultimately be a large determinant of your prices
the end, what it costs you to produce a particu.
menu item will not matter if the price is so high
that no one will buy it. Make sure that your pri
reflect not only the cost of the item but also wh
the competition is charging and what the custo
is willing to spend on an item.

- **Price competitively.** Market-driven prices are
  more responsive to competition. Menu items
  that are common in an area (hamburgers,
  chicken sandwiches and French fries) and can
  purchased at many restaurants and have to be
  priced competitively.

- **Signature dishes.** Focus on prices that are
  demand driven; profitability will be higher. Thes
  may be signature items or simply items that are
  hot food trends.

- **Location and atmosphere are also important
  in determining menu prices.** If you buy red
  snapper in Seattle, the price you expect to pay
  a customer is greater than what you would exp
  to pay for the same dinner in Athens, Georgia.
  Likewise, if you purchase a grilled chicken
  sandwich at a restaurant with table service, you
  expect to pay more than if you get this meal at
  drive-through restaurant.

- **Keep an eye on the competition.** Check out w
  the competition is charging. If you are serving t
  exact same item as the diner down the street fo
  $3 more, you will invariably lose customers to t
  other diner, all other things being equal.

Customers' willingness to pay. This is very important when making pricing decisions. All the other factors make no difference if your customer thinks your prices are too high for what they are receiving. Remember, your customers aren't concerned with your costs. They are concerned with getting their money's worth when they dine out.

Indirect Factors Can Help Increase Profits

ertain factors may give you a competitive edge, allowing you to charge more than the competition your products. For instance, if you operate a steak se that serves prime beef and all the other steak ses in town serve choice and select, you are able harge more for your product because of the higher lity. Other factors may allow you to charge more (or) as well. If your steak house has lush decorations the service is impeccable, or if you have off-street alet parking, you offer amenities that allow you to rge higher prices than some of your competition may ble to. Make the most of the following:

Plate presentation. Introduce flair! Good plate presentations will allow higher prices than a plate that was given no thought as to its appearance. If the customer is served a plate that looks good, with thought given to garnishes, arrangement and color, he or she will be willing to pay more than if the food is thrown on the plate and hurried out of the kitchen.

Serve food on china and use nice glassware. It will add value to the meal, enabling you to charge more than if you served meals on plastic or in Styrofoam.

- **Atmosphere and décor.** Consider remodeling y[o]
  restaurant if it has not been updated for a num[]
  of years. Would just a fresh coat of paint spruce
  up your dining room and make it an attractive,
  comfortable place for a meal?

- **Cleanliness.** Customers do not want to eat in a
  restaurant that is dirty, nor do they want to eat
  with utensils that have not been properly cleane[]
  Keep a regular cleaning and pest-control schedu[]
  Make sure your restaurant is an attractive venu[]

- **Service.** What type of service do you offer? Whil[]
  your customer definitely wants quality food, goo[]
  service is just as important.

- **Table service.** Focus more on table service. It
  always allows you to charge higher menu prices
  than carryout service.

- **Location.** Where are you located? This is an
  important factor in determining what you will b[e]
  able to charge. If you are in a middle-class neigl[]
  borhood, you won't want your prices to be on th[]
  cutting edge even if your food is. If you are in a
  more urban environment, you can probably do
  both.

- **What is your customer base?** If your customer[]
  are college students, you know they have limite[d]
  spending budgets. Don't price yourself out of th[e]
  market.

at Your Psychology Teacher Never Told You

ustomer psychology is an indirect pricing factor
that must always be kept in mind. We've all seen
Wal-mart ads with the smiley face cutting the price
s. Prices go from $5.99 to $4.88 or $2.95 to $2.45.
es often end in odd amounts (in restaurants these
unts are usually fives and nines). Psychologically,
se prices are perceived as lower than a price that
s in zero. So, $12.95 is lower than $13.00 in the
tomer's mind. When the difference involves three
our digits, the difference in perception is increased:
95 is much less than $10.00. Consider a few simple
chological truths:

- **Customer perception.** Think about the last time
  you made a major purchase, such as an appliance
  or a car. More than likely when you saw the $995
  sticker, your mind perceived that as $900, or less
  than $1,000, rather than $1,000. Price dishes "just
  under" for maximum profits.

- **"Mental" budget.** Remember, customers tend to
  have a mental budget of their general monthly
  expenditures. Mental accounting plays a role in
  how much a customer is willing to pay. We all keep
  mental tabs on how much money we have, what
  we need for bills that month and how much we can
  spend on entertainment. Most people include their
  grocery money as part of their bills' budget and
  their entertainment money as a separate budget.

- **Convenience.** Generally these days, people eat
  out as a convenience. It becomes a substitute for
  making a meal at home. Or, perhaps, they eat
  out as a social activity – as entertainment on the
  weekend or for special occasions such as birthdays
  and anniversaries. Tap into this convenience
  factor.

- **The experience.** How your customer perceives your restaurant - as an "eating out" for consumption and convenience or a "dining out" social and entertainment purposes - will affect the prices you can charge. Most people are willing to spend more for their special occasion or dining-o experience because this money comes from their entertainment budget. People tend to spend this money more freely. Most of us are willing to try that fancy new restaurant as part of our spouse' birthday present. But, few of us would be willing to spend the budgeted weekly grocery money for a dinner there. Establish how your customers perceive your operation. Are you an "eating out" a "dining out" restaurant?

Categorize Your Establishment

If you operate a fast-food establishment, you're probably an eating-out restaurant. If you operate a fine-dining restaurant, you're probably considered a dining-out establishment to most customers. If you ar a mid-price restaurant, you may fall into either or bot of these categories. How can this information work for you and help you realize greater profits?

- **Consider changing from being an eating-out establishment to being a dining-out establishment.** Increase your revenues by increasing you guest-check averages and your weekend sales.

- **Special offers.** Increase the number of your budget-minded, weeknight customers by offering them special prices. Introduce discount coupons specials, etc.

- **Always bear in mind that everyone compariso**

shops. Whatever your enterprise, customers will always compare like with like. If they try out a new store or restaurant, they'll use the more familiar one as the reference.

* **Check out your competition and see how your menu prices compare.** If your prices are too high, customers won't feel you offer price value and will take their business to the restaurant that offers similar fare at lower prices.

* **Time and place.** Time and place affect customer price tolerance. Bear in mind that both factors affect how much customers are willing to pay for a meal. Someone who buys a hot dog and fries on vacation or at a theme park is a "captive customer." Such customers are more likely to be willing to pay a higher price for the items than if they purchased them from a neighborhood lunch spot.

ality and Pricing

customer determines value by looking at three things: quality, quantity and price. The value restaurant meal increases proportionately with reases in quality of food, service and atmosphere and tion size. Weigh up these factors when pricing your nu:

* **Value is subjective.** It is not the same for all customers at all times. The exact same customer, depending on whether the meal is simply a substitution for a home-cooked, midweek meal or is part of a special celebration with friends, may value the exact same menu item differently.

* **Value.** In general, a lower-priced meal has

value. However, if the customer feels that the foo
or service is poor, the lower price itself will becor
less valuable and the customer will be willing
to pay a higher price to receive a higher-quality
product.

- **Luxury.** Most of us are willing to pay a higher
  price for added luxuries. So, consider, for examp
  presenting steaks on spectacular plates, with a
  side dish of, perhaps, spinach salad and roasted
  new potatoes. The customer will be willing to pa'
  more for it.

- **Quality ingredients.** If you're using high-quality
  ingredients, charge more for them than other
  establishments that use inferior ingredients. You
  food cost will be higher if you use higher quality
  ingredients, but this will be offset by the higher
  price you are able to charge for the product. Also
  while this change may balance itself out, you car
  increase revenues by attracting customers who a
  willing to pay for quality ingredients. This will he
  increase your profits.

Signature Items

If you have a unique way of preparing a menu item,
you will be able to charge more for that particular
item than your competition, simply because you're the
only one fixing that particular item, that particular wa
Maximize on signature items, as follows:

- **"Secret" ingredients.** Introduce a "secret"
  ingredient, such as your very own barbecue sau
  or, maybe, a to-die-for chocolate flourless cake
  for dessert. You can justify charging more for
  something special.

- **Capitalize on your specialty item.** Feature it prominently on your menu and make use of other in-house marketing opportunities so your customers will be aware of the product. You may even want to consider marketing the product as a retail item.

- **Monopoly.** Develop a monopoly on a menu item. Charge more for the item, thus increasing your profits. Watch your sales history closely and see if this increase affects your sales. If it doesn't have a negative impact, this price increase will increase your profits. For example, if you sell your chocolate cake for $4.25, price it at $4.50. If you're selling 35 a night and the price increase isn't impacting your sales, you will increase your monthly revenue by $262.50.

cing Differences between Similar Menu Items

*T*hen you're designing or changing a menu, you will want to look at the prices of similar items on ir menu. There may be an opportunity to increase fits by changing some of these prices. Investigate the owing:

- **Upgrade low-cost items.** For example, if you're serving a roast chicken, your food cost is not very high. If you also offer a chicken tetrazzine, your ingredient list is significantly longer and your labor cost is higher, because this dish takes longer to prepare for service. Now look at the prices of each dish. Let's say the roast chicken is $5.25 and the chicken tetrazzini is $6. Your customers may "upgrade" to the tetrazzine because they think that they're getting a better deal with the more costly item, simply because it's priced so closely to the plain roast chicken.

- **Reduce food costs.** Take the previous example and compare the two dishes. Although the secon dish yields greater profits, you're also incurring more food and labor costs. If one of your goals in menu designing is to decrease food cost, you may want to increase the price difference in thes two dishes. It is likely to impact sales, shifting your customers' attention to the roast chicken. By selling fewer of the high-cost item, you will decrease your food cost. Remember, your main focus should be on the bottom line rather than t effects of menu price increases for any particula item.

- **Review items within the menu categories.** For example, if you're selling strip steak for only $1 more than you're selling a hamburger, your customers will usually choose the steak. In this case, increase the price of the steak. A hamburg is a low-prestige item and can carry a price that only so high. A steak is a higher-prestige item an customers will be willing to pay a somewhat-higl price for that type of item.

- **Substitutions.** Limit the number of items that a substitutions to avoid having a negative impact the sale of other items. When you're reviewing th menu as a whole, certain items can be considere substitution items and other dishes considered complimentary items. Customers may substitute the steak for the hamburger and significantly decrease hamburger sales.

Pricing Add-On Items

In general, prices of add-on items on your menu (appetizers, salads, desserts and beverages) should I

:termined by the average price of your entrées. Also,
·nsider the following add-on issues:

- **Pricing guidelines for add-on items.** A good rule
  of thumb is that your appetizers should be no
  more than 50 percent of your entrée prices. Follow
  the same guidelines for alcoholic beverages if you
  serve them. For example, if your average entrée
  price is $10.95, most bottles of wine on your wine
  list should price no higher than $16.45. Glasses of
  wine should not be higher than $5.50 a glass.

- **Provide a good choice of wines in the medium
  price range.** When it comes to wine, most
  customers are fairly price-conscious. But, they're
  also looking for decent quality. Most will, therefore,
  gravitate towards the middle of a wine list. Be sure
  to offer several interesting bottles of wine in the
  mid-price range.

- **Keep your customer profile in mind.** According
  to a recent article in Restaurant Hospitality (2000),
  the San Francisco Convention and Visitors Bureau
  conducted a survey splitting their sample into two
  groups: foodies (i.e., people who identify themselves
  as having a strong interest in food, cooking and
  dining) and non-foodies. The survey showed that
  foodies would pay up to $26.27 for a bottle of wine,
  whereas non-foodies would not spend more than
  $20.45. For a glass of wine, foodies would spend
  $5.63 and non-foodies would spend $4.85. Bear
  this in mind when pricing your wine.

- **Pricing wine by the glass.** An easy way to decide
  how to price a glass of wine is by looking at your
  bottle prices. Let's say you sell a bottle of wine for
  $18. A bottle contains 750 milliliters (25.4 ounces).
  You can get five 5-ounce glasses out of a bottle.

Divide $18 by 5 and you come up with $3.60 pe
glass.

- **Alcoholic beverage markups.** In general, beer a
wine can be marked up to two to three times the
cost. Mixed drinks can be marked up more, but
the above survey shows, you need to know your
customer base and consider this, before establis
ing drink prices.

The Math and Costing Software

Unfortunately, when it comes to pricing, we have to
do math! The industry generally uses five differen
pricing methods. The pros and cons of each method a
discussed below.

The five methods are as follows:
1. **Food-cost-percentage pricing**

2. **Factor pricing**

3. **Actual-cost pricing**

4. **Gross profit pricing**

5. **Prime-cost pricing**

To use these methods, you will need to gather
certain pieces of information from the following
sources:
- Sales history and daily receipts

- Production sheets

- Profit and loss statements

- **Costing software.** As with many other things, if you have a computer you can buy software that will facilitate your costing profit. Atlantic Publishing offers one such program called NutraCoster. NutraCoster will calculate product cost (including labor, packaging and overhead) and also nutritional content. The program costs about $300 and can be ordered online at www.atlantic-pub.com. Computerized spreadsheets such as Excel can also be customized for use.

d-Cost-Percentage Pricing

his is probably the most widely used method of menu pricing and, more than likely, it will be way you price the majority of your menu items. vever, there may be cases where you think one of the er methods is more appropriate.

alculate cost percentages, use the following figures:

- Target food-cost percentage

- Actual item food cost

- **How it works.** With the food-cost-percentage method, you determine what percentage of sales will be taken by overhead, labor and food cost and what percentage can be profit. Most restaurants want to realize a profit of between 10 and 20 percent, but each establishment is different, so you'll need to determine what your actual and target percentages are.

- **The calculation.** To determine prices with this method, you must know your actual food cost and your target food cost percentage:

Food cost ÷ target food cost percentage = menu pri

- **Example.** Let's say you have a chicken caesar salad on your menu. Its food cost is $1.84 and your establishment's target food cost is 35 perce Therefore: $1.84 ÷ 0.35 = $5.25.

- **Round up or down.** The price in the above example is actually $5.26, but round the last dig to a 5 or a 9 when setting your prices. You could also round up to $5.35, if you feel your custome will pay this amount for this item. Most restaura managers tend to round figures up.

- **Pros.** It's an easy formula to use.

- **Cons.** It doesn't take labor or other costs into co sideration.

Factor Pricing

As with cost-percentage pricing, factoring also uses your overall target food cost (as a percentage) and the particular item's food cost to determine price.

To calculate the price factor, use the following figures:

- Target food-cost percentage
- Actual item food cost

- **How it works.** This method uses a factor that represents food-cost percentage. To determine prices with this method, the food cost is multipli by the pricing factor. The factor will always be th percentage of your desired food cost divided into 100.

- **The calculation.** Let's say you're target food cost is 35 percent. Divide 35 into 100, and you get 2.86 as your factor. By multiplying this number by your food cost, you come up with a price: $100 \div 35 = 2.86$

- **Example.** If the food cost on a dish is $2.67: $2.67 x 2.86 = $7.65.
Food cost x pricing factor = menu price.

- **Pros.** It's an easy method.

- **Cons.** Each individual item will not meet your overall target food cost. Some of your menu items will have a higher cost and some will have a lower cost. Factoring will overprice high-food-cost items and under price low-cost items.

ual-Cost Pricing

his method is used when the menu price is established before the food cost is known. By looking ll other costs, it determines what can be spent of l cost. This method includes profit as part of the 1u price. Catering operations use it when working 1 a customer who has a definite budget that they e to meet. By working back from what the person spend, the manager can determine what kind of 1u they can offer the customer.

alculate actual costs, use the following figures:

- Menu price

- Overhead costs (as a percentage)

- Labor costs (as a percentage)

- Desired profits (as a percentage)

- **How it works.** First you need to determine what percentage of your costs go into overheads and labor and what percentage of sales need to go to profit. Since this equation is expressed as a percentage, overhead, labor, food cost and profit must equal 100 percent: 100% - overhead % - labor % - profit % = food cost %.

- **The calculation.** By looking at your profit and l statement you see that your labor is 30 percent your sales overhead is 20 percent; and you know you are aiming for a 15 percent profit: 100% - 3 - 20% - 15% = 35%. Therefore, you can spend 3 percent of the price you establish on food cost.

- **Example.** Look at your sales history. Let's say you earned $100,000 in a 6-month period. Of th $100,000, $30,000 was spent of labor; $20,000 was spent on overhead expenses; and $15,000 was allocated to profit. That leaves you $35,000 spend on food.

  Let's look at a specific menu item now. Your lasagna sells for $11. Of that $11, $3.30 is spen on labor; $2.20 is spent on overhead; and $1.65 profit. That leaves you $3.85 to spend on food.

- **Pros.** It includes profit in the calculation of the price of each menu item.

- **Cons.** You are working backward from menu pri to food cost, so this method may not be helpful your goal is to come up with menu prices in the first place.

ss Profit Pricing

he gross profit method is designed to enable you to
make a certain amount in profit from each customer.

calculate gross profits, use the following figures:

• Past revenue in dollars

• Past gross profit in dollars

• Past number of customers

• Item's actual food cost

• **How it works.** Let's say your food service
  operation looks at its past month's gross sales
  and you find that you made $80,000 in sales.
  Food cost was $25,600, so your gross profit was
  $54,400. (No costs other than food have been
  subtracted at this point, so this is not net profit.)
  From your guest-check tally you can conclude that
  you served 10,000 customers during that time
  period.

• **The calculation.** Divide the gross profit by the
  number of customers, and an average gross profit
  of $5.44 per customer is established: **Gross profit**
  (**$54,400**) ÷ **number of customers** (10,000) =
  average gross profit per customer ($5.44).

  • Next establish your food cost from your stan-
    dardized recipe.

  • This added to the gross profit determines your
    selling price:
    Food cost + average gross profit = selling price.

• **Example.** Say your lasagna's food cost is $3.85:
  $3.85 + $5.44 = $9.29.

- **Pros.** You are assured of making a predetermine
  amount of money on each customer. It works we
  when customer counts are predictable.

- **Cons.** Hard to adjust for any major changes in
  business or customer counts. It may be more
  adaptable for institutional operations like hospit:
  and schools than for commercial establishments.
  Does not take the cost of labor or other expenses
  into account.

Prime Cost Pricing

Items on your menu will differ with regards to how
much labor is involved in their production. Homem:
soups and desserts, for instance, involve quite a bit
more labor than premade items. This method allows t
price to reflect this labor cost.

- **Calculate labor costs.** Labor expenditure can b
  determined by noting the length of time that ea(
  item takes to prepare. This labor figure should
  include the time taken assembling ingredients
  and utensils, washing, chopping, peeling, mixin,
  preliminary cooking (such as blanching) and
  cleaning. The labor cost is determined by taking
  this amount of time and multiplying it by the
  employee's hourly wage:

  **Employee wage x amount of time to prepare
  labor cost of producing item**

- **Labor cost of individual servings.** In order
  to determine a labor cost for each serving of a
  particular item, simply divide the above numbei
  by the number of portions. When this amount i

added to the food cost, you come up with your prime food cost.

calculate prime costs, use the following figures:

• Total labor cost as a percentage

• Labor cost for preparing item

• Actual item food cost

• Target food cost as percentage

• **How it works.** Look at your menu and determine which items require an extensive amount of labor in the production process. Then determine the labor used to prepare each specific menu item and add the item's food cost to the labor cost to get a total: **food cost + labor cost = item cost.**

• **Next.** Determine what percentage the labor cost for preparing the item is of your total labor percentage. This number will be expressed as a percentage. Add the item's labor percentage to your target food cost (expressed as a percentage) to come up with the prime food cost percentage.

• **Finally.** Divide the total item cost by the prime food cost percentage and you get the menu selling price.

• **Example.** Your menu includes meat lasagna. It takes your prep cook 1.5 hours to prepare two trays of 12 servings. Your prep cook is paid $8 an hour. (Since the line cook does not have to do anything but reheat the lasagna that labor does not have to be figured in). Labor for this item is $12. For each portion the cost is 50 cents: $8 x 1.5 = $12 and $12 ÷ 24 = $0.50.

- **Item labor cost.** By looking at your financial statements you know that your total labor is 25 percent, so you figure out that the labor for this item is 8 percent. Add this percentage to your desired food cost (say 37 percent) for the prime food cost percentage: 8% + 37% = 45%

- **Suggested menu price.** Direct labor percentage + desired food cost percentage = prime food-cost percentage. Now, add the direct labor per portion (50 cents) to the food cost (say $4) and divide th by the prime food cost percentage (45 percent). This will give you a suggested menu price: Direc labor per portion + food cost per portion ÷ prime food cost percentage = suggested menu price: $0.50 + $4 ÷ .45 = $10. In reality, this would probably be adjusted to $9.95.

- **Pros.** It can include cost for labor on items that require a significant amount of labor in the preparation.

- **Cons.** It is a complicated method to use. It shou only be used on items with a high labor cost.

Salad Bar Pricing

Pricing for a salad bar is different from pricing for regular items. You can either price the bar as "all-you-can-eat" or by the ounce. Most restaurants, schools, hospitals and grocery stores seem to be mov to the per-ounce pricing method. The following provid a simple guideline:

- **To price an all-you-can-eat bar.** First, figure ou the cost of all the items on the bar. Then, keep track of how much of each item you put out at the beginning of a service period. After the service period, measure and/or weigh what you have left. The difference between what you set out and what you have left is what was consumed.

- **Check register reports.** For example, if you set out $1,000 worth of product and you had $500 left at the end of the service period, you sold $500 worth of food. Now, check your register reports or guest checks and see how many customers went through the salad bar.

- **Analyze one week's worth of information.** Keep track of this information for at least a week and then use the information to come up with an average price. If, over a week, you sold $2,500 worth of food at the salad bar and 600 people had salad, you would want to charge $4.25 for the all-you-can-eat salad bar.

- **Pricing by the ounce.** Many supermarkets price takeout salad this way. This is a little more complicated, but pricing this way also relieves a lot of the headaches associated with an all-you-can-eat bar, including how to do carryout, people sharing plates, etc. The most straightforward way to price a by-the-ounce salad bar is to average the costs. Let's say you have the following ingredients at the following costs per pound on the bar:

Lettuce	$1.75
Tomatoes	$2.50
Carrots	$1.79
Chickpeas	$0.56
Cucumbers	$0.75
Shredded cheese	$4.35

1.75 + 2.50 + 1.79 + 0.56 + 0.75 + 4.35 = $11.7
per pound

Divide $11.70 by 16 to come up with your ounc
price: $11.70 ÷ 16 = $0.73.

- **A word of caution.** From the above example, yo
  could price your salad bar at 73 cents per ounce
  But take a good look at this price and make
  sure it will cover your costs. Salad bar items are
  extremely variable in weights and costs (think o
  bean sprouts versus cheese). Once you have cor
  up with your average price, you can manipulate
  this to make it fit your cost structure and marke
  influences.

CHAPTER SIX

MARKETING YOUR MENU (& YOUR RESTAURANT)

ernal Marketing and Suggestive Selling

iternal marketing refers to techniques used once he customer is inside the establishment. The goal of ernal marketing in restaurants is to figure out how to ike and keep your customers happy and how to make :m repeat customers. Repeat business is the key to ilizing profits - consistently.

re are some methods of internal marketing:

- Put a copy of your menu in the window to attract foot traffic.

- Use table tents.

- Use dessert carts.

- Introduce chef's tables.

- **Suggestive selling.** Suggestive selling is an excellent marketing tool. Train all your servers how to make menu suggestions when they take orders. Remember, suggestive selling is a verbal expansion of your written menu. Try the following approaches to suggestive selling:

  - **Encourage customer/server interaction.** For example, you can have servers tell customers about daily specials or desserts. This approach often provides customers with the information and opinions that will help them decide what satisfy them. It also helps make the interaction between server and customer a little more personal and friendly.

- **Extras.** Have your servers suggest something in addition to what the customer may normal order, such as an appetizer or dessert. The simple question, "Would you like an appetizer this evening?" followed by, "The shrimp cocktail is very good tonight," will increase your appetizer sales for the evening.

- **Product knowledge.** To do a good job at suggestive selling, servers must have knowledge of the products. Hold training sessions that allow servers to taste wines and food. Tell them how the items are made. If you are running a special, let the servers see and taste the special before service begins.

Promotions

Promotions can be handled any number of ways, but above all, offer something different. People will go to your restaurant if you offer something they can't get anywhere else. This may be a menu item or something else. Here are a couple of examples: Miami University Ohio recently built a new student dining hall that offers fresh-made noodle and stir-fry dishes. At this particular hall, the chef prepares the dishes up front, chatting with customers as their food is cooked. The owner of a local pizza restaurant was known for balancing things on his nose. Customers would come in to eat simply to watch him balance a football helmet, a sword or a chair on the bridge of his nose. (You probably don't want to try this second example, but you get the idea!) Be creative and

e what innovative ideas you can come up with! Here
e some ideas to promote your menu:

- **Table tents.** Cheap to produce, table tents are among one of the most popular ways of promoting your menu.

- **Appetizer trays.** If you are adding a new appetizer to the menu, have one of your servers take a tray of the appetizer into your front area and serve the customers waiting to be seated.

- **Trying to increase your dessert sales** for the month? Create a contest for your servers: the first one to sell 15 desserts gets a bottle of wine.

- **Start serving brunch.** When the server gives the customer his or her dinner check, included a coupon for brunch as well.

- **Free drawing.** Invite customers to drop their business cards into a fishbowl. Hold a drawing once a week. The winner receives a free lunch for two.

- **Use these business cards to create an e-mail mailing list.** Send out e-mails when you have specials or promotions, or promote your catering business this way.

- **Create T-shirts with your restaurant's name and logo.** Sell these at the hostess stand.

- **Offer an express lunch special.** Target business clientele who need a quick lunch.

- **Add entertainment after the dinner rush.** This will bring people in who will drink and have appetizers or desserts.

External Promotions

For external promotions, you need to be careful. Make sure you know exactly what needs promoting before spending your revenue on advertising. Advertising is expensive and there's no guarantee it will succeed. If you have a plan and a goal in mind, however, your chances of a successful marketing experience are much greater! Do your homework before you spend your money! Here are some ideas for external promotion:

- **Donate food to a local public radio fund drive.** This will give you free advertising on the station when they thank the people who donated food.

- **Visit your local chamber of commerce.** All cities have festivals, parades and other events. See how you can involve your restaurant.

- **Local advertising.** If you have an adequate advertising budget, place ads in newspapers, on the radio or on television.

- **Set up cooking demonstrations at a local mall**

- **Talk to area schools about conducting a tour of your facility as a school field trip.** The local newspaper might want to cover the event.

Coupons

One of the most popular forms of external marketing is the use of coupons. Coupons are everywhere these days. All types of restaurants offer coupons from fast-food establishments to fine-dining. Join the bandwagon. Coupons are used for two reasons: to

rease sales and increase awareness. The real goal is
get the customer who came in on a coupon to come
:k. If people only come in when they have coupons,
ı may run into problems with this advertising
ategy. You may find that your advertising costs are
her than your earnings. Consider the following:

- **Choose the type of coupon that suits your establishment.** You need to be careful with what type of coupons you use and what your coupons say. You can't make any profits if you are just giving away food!

- **Identify your goals.** Coupons fall into two broad categories: unconditional and conditional. Which type is more likely to entice your local clientele?

- **Unconditional coupons are those you often see in pizza ads - "buy one get one free."** Is this type of coupon going to encourage loyalty?

- **Conditional coupons have some sort of restriction placed on them.** This restriction may be that it can't be used on weekends, or it may only apply up to a certain dollar amount. You set the restriction.

- **Why use coupons?** If you decide to try coupons, you need to determine what you want these coupons to achieve.
    - Do you want to increase sales at a particular time of the day?

    - Do you want to increase the sales of a particular item?

    - Do you want to increase the number of customers you have as a whole?

How to Use Coupons

There are numerous ways to get coupons to potential customers. Once you've reached your target audience, you also need to track coupon usage. If you don't, you'll never be able to gauge the coupon's effectiveness. You won't know if it's an effective marketing tool or if you're achieving the goals you established. Bear in mind the following strategies:

- **Direct mailing.** Check with your local post office. You can "purchase" zip codes to use for bulk mailing. If you choose this method, you must first determine where you customers are coming from and then you'll want to market to those zip codes.

- **If you manage a smaller restaurant with a tight budget, you can use flyers.** A local pizzeria hires teenagers in the summer. The manager prints several hundred flyers, then drives the teenagers around in his truck. The kids deliver flyers to all the houses in his area. This strategy is especially effective just before the weekend, and it always results in an increase in volume immediately after the coupons have been distributed.

- **Consider advertising in local coupon publications.**

- **Student clientele.** If you are located near a college, you can place coupons in the college paper that will be distributed throughout the campus and dormitories.

nature Items as a Marketing Tool

ignature items make excellent marketing tools.
By definition, a signature item is an item for
ch you are recognized. In Cincinnati, several local
aurant chains have signature items. For example,
itgomery Inn is known for its barbecue sauce and
line is known for its three-way and five-way chili.
signature item creates a monopoly for you. When
istomer says to a friend, "Oh you've got to try the
ried lobster bisque at the Inn on the Hill," that friend
only come to your establishment to get that dish.
v, the trick is to make the public aware of the dish.
it's where marketing comes into play.

- **Advertise your signature item.** Often word of
  mouth is the best external marketing, but you can
  also use your advertising budget to feature your
  signature item in your ads.

- **Positioning.** Internally, marketing revolves around
  how the item is placed on the menu, how well
  your staff promotes the item and how well you use
  other internal marketing devices, such as table
  tents, dessert carts and specialty menus.

- **Graphics.** Feature your signature item
  prominently on the menu. Use boxes or graphic
  elements to draw the customers' attention. Your
  servers are also instrumental in drawing attention
  to signature items. Make sure they know how the
  item is prepared and how it tastes. In addition,
  make sure they are suggesting it to customers.

- **If you don't have a signature item, maybe it's
  time to create one.** Work with your chef and see
  what you can create. Pay attention to current food
  trends when working on this. Also pay attention

to ingredients. You don't want a signature dish
with ingredients that are difficult to find half of
year. Finally, make sure that your dish is going
be profitable. Creating a spectacular dish that s
like crazy is not going to do you any good if you
cannot make a profit on it.

- **Maybe you have a signature dish and don't
  realize it.** Does everyone love the lentil soup? D
  you sell more duck egg rolls than anything else
  the appetizer menu? Look at your sales history.
  Maybe by adding an extra flair to an existing di\
  you can create a signature dish.

Restaurant Web site

Hosting your own Web site can be a great,
inexpensive way to market yourself! It may be
something you can create on your own, or you can h\
a company to design and manage the site for you. Be
in mind the following:

- **First, ask your staff.** Before going to a professional to create a Web site, you may want to as\
  your employees. Many restaurants have a large
  college population on staff. One of your employe\
  may be able to design and host your site at a m\
  competitive price.

- **Use a professional.** Gizmo Graphics is a profes\
  sional Web site design company that specializes
  the food service industry; they can be contacted
  www.gizwebs.com.

• **Information.** Include the following kinds of information on your Web site:

  • Directions and a map

  • An easy way to make reservations

  • Your menu

  • Any retail items you want to promote

• **List your Web site.** Investigate having your Web site listed with one of the major search engines, such as Lycos, Yahoo or Google. Working with the search engine's rules can be tricky, so you may want to look into hiring someone for this. You can get more information at www.wilsonweb.com and www.webpromote.com.

• **Alternatives.** If you decide that your own Web site isn't for you, look into placing your menu on a local paper's site. Most city papers have a Web site with an entertainment section. Contact the editor and see how you can get your menu included.

• **Get listed on other Web sites.** If your restaurant attracts tourists as customers, find out how to advertise or how to get listed on sites such as www.restaurants.com, www.epinions.com and www.trianglerestaurants.com.

rent Food Trends

order to market your establishment successfully s an enterprise, you must be aware of current food ids in the industry as well as in your particular lity. This knowledge will help you make the right keting and pricing decisions.

- **Go with the current trends.** Consider introduc
  ethnic dishes, specifically Mexican, Southwester
  Asian, Indian, Caribbean and Cajun.

- **The takeout market.** Possibly include more fas
  food items and more mid-price dinner items tha
  only need reheating.

- **More lean and healthy menu choices.** Always
  winner!

- **Demonstrate an interest in fresh ingredients**
  and homemade products.

- **Take a look at the Restaurant Industry
  Forecast for 2002.** It's available from the Natio
  Restaurant Association and contains informatio
  concerning forecasted restaurant industry sales
  and forecasted trends.

CHAPTER SEVEN

OPERATIONAL CONTROLS & MENU MANAGEMENT

:hen Space

he control process allows managers to establish
standards and standard procedures. It is used
rain all employees to follow those standards and
cedures, monitor performance and take appropriate
on to correct any deviations from the established
cedures. Kitchen organization is a major consid-
tion when setting up operational controls and
adards.

- **Review the available facilities.** Before you create
  or redesign a menu, you should take a good look
  at your kitchen and analyze exactly what it can
  provide. Look at the following aspects:

  - What is the kitchen size?

  - How many stations are there?

  - How many kitchen employees do you have
    working the dinner or lunch rush?

  - How much and what types of equipment do you
    have?

  - How much storage room do you have?

  - Is your kitchen getting orders out in a timely
    manner?

- **Review your menu to make the most of your facilities.** If employees are getting in each other way at certain workstations during rush periods consider a serious menu overhaul. Or, maybe yo menu is appetizer heavy, and you only have one employee at that station that also has to help th grill cook. If you want to keep all the appetizers, you may need to think about adding additional staff.

- **Extra staff during busy periods.** If, after reviewing the menu, you need to bring in extra staff, you may want to raise your appetizer price to compensate. If you think your appetizer sales will decrease with a price increase, you may wai to eliminate some of the choices. This way your appetizer cook can get things out on time and correctly. This more efficient service may even increase your appetizer sales even though there may be fewer choices.

- **Monitor current procedures.** When contemplat ing a menu change, first watch your kitchen as they prepare the current menu. Are there ways which you could change an item's preparation o ingredients that would strengthen the menu? Ai there ways to simplify preparation procedures ii order to lower costs? All of these questions need to be considered when designing or redesigning menu.

Purchasing

As a food service manager, you forecast sales revenues and relate these calculations to what yo should purchase, how to store it and how to prepare

r menu has a direct impact on all of these decisions.
rder for your pricing system to work and make
fits for you, other systems in your operation must
) be working properly. These other systems include
chasing, production, training and security.

- **Purchasing procedures.** These procedures should include creating written purchasing specifications for every product and selecting good, reliable purveyors. Your purchasing program should do three things:

  1. Allow you to purchase the required items at prices that meet your food cost goals.

  2. Maintain control over your existing inventory.

  3. Establish a set of procedures to be sure that you receive quality product at the best price.

- **Purchasing responsibility.** Either take on the purchasing yourself or assign a specific employee to do it. Make sure that this person keeps current with ever-changing food prices.

- **Price check different vendors.** Sometimes you may find that one vendor is less expensive than another for a while, and then this may shift. Keep current with competing vendors' prices.

- **Minimize food loss in storage.** Keep frozen food at 0° F; food in dry storage areas should be stored at temperatures around 50° F. Keep food in dry storage on shelves at least 6 inches from the floor and the wall. Make sure the staff is storing raw meat on shelves below raw produce, and be sure that fresh fish is being kept on ice in the refrigerator to maintain the proper temperature of 30-34° F degrees.

- **Stock rotation.** If you don't have a stock rotati*
  system in place, you may be losing product due
  spoilage.

- **Introduce a receiving policy for receiving ord**
  from vendors. Remember, it's easy to "lose"
  products in this part of your operation. Let's sa*
  for example, you have no one specifically assign
  to check in orders. Normally one of your line co
  will do it. Let's also say that one day your order
  late and arrives in the middle of lunch rush. No
  one can check the order for accuracy, so someo*
  just signs for it in a hurry. If this happens, it is
  virtually impossible to correct any mistakes at t
  time. Furthermore, if your line cooks don't get t
  put the order away until several hours later, you
  will lose product because it has sat out too long
  and is now unsafe to serve.

- **Storeroom access.** Only allow particular
  employees to retrieve or store items. Institute a
  sign-in/sign-out procedure. By keeping track of
  what comes in and goes out of your inventory, y*
  can minimize losses attributed to theft, waste a*
  overportioning.

Purchasing Specifications

By creating purchasing specifications, you can con
which items you purchase and you can maintain
product consistency. This information is extremely
important if you have more than one person that doe
ordering in your operation. You need to record the
following basic information:

- **Purchasing specifications.** They state the exact requirements for the amount and quality of items purchased. These specifications should include:
  - Product name
  - Quantity to be purchased (designated with correct unit such as pounds, can size, etc.)
  - Indication of grade, if applicable
  - Unit by which prices are quoted
  - What the product will be used to produce

- **Introduce a record sheet.** Make it readily available for all your employees. They need to be sure that they're ordering the correct items, in the correct amounts. You're also more likely to attain your desired food cost by keeping these records and maintaining purchasing controls. Keeping your food cost down will help you to maximize profits from your menu prices. The following form illustrates an example of a purchasing specification form:

ITEM	QTY.	UNIT	PRICING UNIT	UNIT PRICE	AMOUNT
nned diced nato	4	#10 cans	Case	$10.83	$43.32
edded volone cheese	10	lbs	lb	$4.55	$45.50

Purchasing and Inventory Software

Purchasing and inventory software is readily availab
to restaurant operators. Many larger organiza-
tions are using inventory-control software that saves a
significant amount of time and money. Most managers
are used to the monthly grind, standing in the walk-in
counting eggs, butter pats and frozen chickens. With
inventory-control software, managers can use a laser
scanner, similar to the ones used in grocery stores, to
scan bar codes. The software can also be linked to you
distributors, and you can place your orders electroni-
cally based on the inventory.

Software Vendors

- **Visit the National Restaurant Association's
  Web site** at www.restaurant.org for vendors of
  this software (as well as many other products).
  Take a trip to their annual National Restaurant
  Association Exhibit each year in Chicago to see
  all the latest products available in the restaurant
  industry.

- **You can see one version of the inventory
  software on the Johnson Technologies Web
  site** at www.johnsontech.com. According to their
  Web site, their EZ Stock can be purchased for
  $25 a month per module for a minimum of one
  year. Atlantic Publishing (www.atlantic-pub.com)
  also has a software program, called ChefTec,
  for inventory control, recipes, menu costing and
  nutritional analysis. For information on this
  software package, you can call them at 800-541-
  1366.

- **Another Web site of interest is www.foodprofi**
  com. This site was established for the collection

and distribution of product information for the food industry and is part of an initiative called Efficient Foodservice Response (EFR). Distributors pay to list their products on this site. It provides over 65,000 items and has the most up-to-date product information available, including serving suggestions, nutritional information, cooking instructions and ingredient statements. EFR is an industry-wide initiative to improve efficiency in the purchasing process. To find out more about EFR, log on to www.efr-central.com.

oduction

The standardized recipe is crucial in controlling food cost. Together with the production sheet, these are cessary tools when determining menu prices. Physical oduction should also be considered when looking at nu changes. Watch your kitchen operation to see w things are working. You may need to buy some w equipment or rearrange your labor schedule to plement some of the changes that you want. Focus rticularly on the following:

- **Labor.** Are you scheduling the appropriate amount of labor for shifts and pre-prep work?

- **Recipes.** Be sure staff members are using the standardized recipes and production sheets.

- **Inventory controls.** Do you have strict inventory controls in place? Is your staff familiar with inventory procedures?

- **Invest in labor-saving equipment.** You'll be able to pay for the equipment in no time with the money that you will save on labor.

- **An important part of the production process is keeping food safe.** Make sure you have Hazard Analysis Critical Control Points (HACCP) procedures in place and train your kitchen staff in food safety. Many culinary programs offer sanitation classes that provide state certification in sanitation. Visit www.atlantic-pub.com for complete training information and food-safety products.

- **Simple things.** Here are a few simple things to do now to be sure your employees are keeping your food items safe:

  - **Buy and use separate color-coded cutting boards** for raw meats and vegetables to prevent cross-contamination.

  - **Make sure employees wash their hands.**

  - **Use a sanitizer to clean surfaces** that come into contact with food.

Presentation

Plate presentation is an important element of any menu item. Food that is presented well is perceived to have more value by the customer, and your prices f well-plated food can be on the higher side of the price continuum. Consider the following:

ee elements comprise plate presentation:

1. Dish type and size

2. Portion size

3. Garnish

- **Provide the appropriate plate sizes for menu items.** Otherwise, kitchen staff may be prone to overportioning. For example, if a salad that should be plated on a salad dish is put on a dinner plate, the pantry person is likely to add more salad so that the dish does not swallow up the item. Include plate size information on your standardized recipe.

- **Portion size should also be included on your standardized recipe.** Consistent portioning is important to customer satisfaction, especially for your regulars. Your customers may order the same dish many times. It's important that each time it comes out of the kitchen it looks and tastes the same and is consistent. Since most restaurants have various people working in the kitchen, you must put controls in place so that everyone creates the same dish the same way each and every time. Consider McDonald's Corporation restaurants: regardless of where you buy a cheeseburger - from any unit anywhere in the world - it will always look, taste and weigh the same and be packaged and presented in the same amount of time. You can expect it to be served the same way each and every time.

- **Garnish is often overlooked in recipes and in presentation.** For minimal cost, garnishes can add to the appearance of your plates. Garnish can be anything, from simple chopped parsley to sauces drizzled across the plate in a decorative manner. It's the slice of lemon on top of your salmon or the cheese croutons in the soup. Need some ideas? There is a wide selection of great books on garnishing at www.atlantic-pub.com.

- **Arrangement.** Along with the actual garnish ingredients, think about how you want the food to be arranged on the plate. Factors to consider when arranging a plate are:

  - **Layout.** Think about where you want the customer to focus. Usually a plate consists of meat, a starch and a vegetable. Most times you want the customer to focus on the most expensive item on the plate (this will enhance the perceived value of the meal). The main element of the plate is usually the meat, so you would usually want your customer to focus on that item.

  - **Balance.** Take the balance of the plate into consideration. Balance refers to the weight of the items on the plate.

  - **Line.** Line is also important, because a strong line has strong eye appeal. A strong line helps to draw the customer's eye to the plate.

  - **Dimension/height.** Dimension, or height, also adds to a plate's appeal. Use molds to mound potatoes or rice and lean meat up against these mounds to create height and a three-dimensional plate. Don't overdo the height factor, however. You don't want to overwhelm the taste of the food itself by the presentation. Do not overstack or overportion a plate.

- **Color.** This is important in plate presentation. Try to get maximum eye appeal. Perhaps top your salmon with some red pepper curls or chopped chives.

- **Maneuverability.** Keep in mind that the customer is eventually going to eat the masterpiece that you have just created. Don't make it difficult to reach around garnishes or to cut into the food.

- **Overall appearance.** For example, rather than just putting the sliced roast pork beside the mashed potatoes and the green beans, tie the pieces together. Place the mound of potatoes in the center of the plate and fan the slices of pork around it leaning against the mound. Tie the green beans into a bundle with a steamed chive and angle them on the other side of the potatoes. Think of the plate as a canvas and see what you can create.

- **Serviceability of china.** Balance durability with aesthetics.

everages

Just as you have controls for purchasing, storing and producing food items, you need to have controls over lcoholic beverages if your establishment sells them. ear in mind a few basic issues:

- **Recipes.** Stick to standard recipes for drink mixtures to maintain quality standards and to control costs.

- **Product list.** List all beverage product names in your purchasing controls. The list should include the quantities in which the products are purchased, indication of proof and the unit by which prices are quoted.

- **Presentation.** Beverage controls should also det: presentation, including what type of glassware tc use and any drink garnishes.

- **Guidelines.** Bar and beverage procedural manuals on bar inventory, how to control theft, cost control, recipe manuals, and bar software a available at www.atlantic-pub.com (or request a free catalog at 800-814-1132).

Labor Controls

Labor is one of the costs that you may be able to reduce in order to increase your menu profits. A few suggestions:

- **Introduce premade items.** Shift from some scrat(items to premade items to cut down on prep time.

- **Cut back on staffing during slow periods.**

- **Allocate the right staff to the right job.** Shift some of the prep work from higher-paid employee: to those that make a lower hourly wage.

- **Streamline your kitchen to make it more efficient.** This may include buying new equipmen and/or moving existing equipment.

- **Train your kitchen staff.** Not just as a one-shot, when they take up employment at your establishme hold regular training sessions. Everyone benefits.

• **Hire cooks with experience.**

rvice

ervice has a direct, significant impact on the prices
you can charge. Restaurants that offer better service
1 charge more for their menu items, because the
vice increases, the meal's value in the customers'
ception. Style of service must also be kept in mind
en establishing prices. Here are some things that are
portant in making the customers' experience at your
taurant a positive one from beginning to end:

• **First impressions.** The customer expects good
service, and many places offer this. You have to go
the extra step and make service special. The first
person that the customer encounters will make
an impression to the last, so make sure you train
your employees on how to greet, serve and interact
with your customers. Often you may not be on the
floor, so it's important that each employee knows
what is expected and gives the customers clear
signals that they are your guests.

• **Greetings.** Employees should greet the customer
with a smile and pleasant tone of voice.

• **Make sure management is visible.** Stop by the
table to check on customers during their meal.
Send the message that you are concerned about
their satisfaction.

• **Have your servers treat regulars like family.** If a
customer always comes in on Tuesdays and orders
the Red Beans and Rice, then asks for Tabasco,
have the server there with Tabasco in hand before
the customer has to ask.

- **Let your servers taste menu items.** They will [] able to provide better service if they can give the customer information and opinions on the menu offerings.

- **Listen to your customers.** Act on suggestions [] comments to make your establishment the best [] can be.

- **Consider introducing a point-of-sale (POS) system.** Not only will this allow you to reduce labor costs and speed up service, but it will also allow you to capture information about your customer. Use this information. By linking the POS system to your credit card reading device, [] are able to collect demographic information, suc[] as spending habits, birthdays, etc. This system can do everything from reminding your servers [] take drinks to a table to tracking inventory. Sho[] around and pay special attention to support wh[] looking at POS systems.

- **Remember that the customer is always right.**

Employee Training

A great deal of your time as a food service manager [] spent in managing your employees. This includes everything from recruitment and hiring to training an[] retraining. In order to manage your menu and realize[] the profits that you desire, you must be sure your employees are trained.

- **New employees.** When a new employee comes into your establishment, you should make certa[] that he or she is given an orientation. Make sur[] the new employee is given copies of all restaura[]

polices and a written job description.

- **Ongoing training.** New employees are not the only employees that need training. Provide continual, scheduled training for your entire staff. You must have your staff trained in order to maintain quality standards and to keep your costs under control. This, in turn, will lead to realizing greater profits. For complete training resources for the hospitality industry, visit www.atlantic-pub.com.

- **Training goals.** When you undertake a training program, have goals in mind. What do you want to accomplish with each training session? Who should attend the training?

- **Present information in a relevant manner.** Call a company-wide meeting perhaps, and give the information in a lecture format. Use demonstrations, videotapes and tests. If you are designing a new menu that will have several new items, perhaps you could have a meeting to describe the menu. Follow up with a tasting and role playing. Let the staff pretend to describe the new items to other staff acting as customers.

- **Decrease employee turnover rate.** Not only will you have a more knowledgeable staff if you commit to a training program, but you'll also decrease your employee turnover rate, develop employee loyalty and reduce the number of customer complaints.

- **Be positive.** As often as you can, reward for good behavior. Positive reinforcement is always better than negative. Your employees will respond to it better.

- **Lead by example.** Remember, the best training [you] can offer your employees is to set a good exampl[e.]

- **External training.** Send your staff on external training courses. The National Restaurant Association offers courses in management and f[ood] safety and the American Culinary Federation off[ers] certification for chefs. To find out more about chef certification, visit the American Culinary Federation Web site at www.acfchefs.org.

Other training resources include:

- **Educational Institute of the American Hotel and Motel Association**
  800-349-0299, www.ei-ahma.org

- **National Restaurant Association**
  800-765-2122, www.restaurant.org

- **Atlantic Publishing**
  800-814-1132, www.atlantic-pub.com

Internal Security

Employee theft is a reality and it can have an impact on costs, profits and menu pricing. It's been estima[ted] that businesses lose between $5 and $10 billion each year due to employee theft. In restaurants, employee th[eft] accounts for approximately 75 percent of a restaurant'[s] inventory shortages. When we say employee theft, we are talking about anything from outright stealing from the cash register, to not writing up a guest check for ar[n] employee meal, to slipping friends a few free drinks.

Types of internal theft.
While this list is not comprehensive, here are some o[f] the typical types of internal theft of which you shoul[d] aware:

- **A cashier not recording a sale** on the cash register or under-ringing the sale and pocketing the difference.

- **Lost checks** where the money is actually pocketed.

- **Altering checks.** Charging guests higher than the menu price, but only cashing out the correct amount and pocketing the difference.

- **Switching checks.** A server gives a customer a check for another table that is more than what they owe. If the person pays, the server pockets the difference.

- **Underpouring drinks** or reporting drinks as spilled or returned drinks are sold but not rung up.

- **Recording drink sales as bottle sales.**

- **Payroll theft.**

- **Also be aware of theft from suppliers and vendors.** Make sure there is enough time to check all incoming orders. Watch for close relationships between employees and suppliers that could lead to collusion.

- **Employees eating food they haven't paid for.**

- **After-hours drinking on the restaurant's tab.**

- **Recording information on guest checks incorrectly** for friends' meals.

- **Walking off with inventory items.**

Reduce the Risks of Theft

So what are some of the things that you can do to minimize your risk? While there are several strategies available to help you in the battle against employee theft, the best strategy is to communicate with your employees and create a positive workplace environment. By motivating your employees to do a g job and by showing your employees respect, you are using your best tools to deter internal theft. After all, you show your employees respect, they will value yo an employer and not want to steal from you in the fir place. In the meantime, however, always be realistic. Bear in mind the following issues:

- **First - know who you're hiring.** Check referen Verify past employment.

- **Conduct a security audit of your restaurant.** Discover your vulnerable points.

- **Establish a list of the most valuable goods in your inventory**. Maintain a continual, simple audit of these goods.

- **Separate duties.** Introduce a system of checks and balances in each area of your operation.

- **Security.** Keep your receiving and inventory are secure.

- **Tighten up receiving procedures.** Check quantities and quality of goods coming in again invoices and original orders.

- **Have production controls in place.** Standardi recipes and make sure the right size of equipme is available. This will help alleviate the problem of cooks overportioning for friends, coworkers, etc.

- **Employee meals.** Make sure you have an employee meal policy and that this information is communicated to all employees.

- **Personal possessions.** Don't let cashiers store their purses or bags by the register.

- **Have specific procedures for the cashier to follow.** For example, if the cashier rings up a void, the manager must sign it.

- **Provide accountability with cash drawers.** Only one person other than you on a shift should have access to a drawer.

- **Audit your guest checks and transactions.** Do this on a regular basis and make weekly and monthly comparisons.

- **Guest checks.** Use numbered guest checks and do a nightly tally.

- **Keys.** Guard against the theft or duplication of keys.

- **Watch trash removal.** Often an employee will take a stolen item out with the trash and retrieve it later. Have a supervisor or another person go with employees when they are taking out the trash. Use clear garbage bags. Limit parking at the trash area.

- **Consider introducing closed-circuit TV cameras.**

- **Deposit all cash daily.** Keep up with your sales paperwork on a daily basis.

- **The consequences.** Make sure employees know the consequences of employee theft, including th possibility of criminal prosecution.

External Theft

External theft is also a factor in cost control, so you want to have safety mechanisms in place to minimize your risk in this area as well. Restaurants are often targets because of the large amount of cash hand and the late operating hours. Check these entry exit points and make sure they are secure:

- **Doors.** If you have glass doors, consider installii bars over the glass. Also, make sure that your back doors are secure. These may be left open accidentally after a delivery, or employees may prop open a door for cool air during the shift.

- **Windows.** Make sure you have locks that functi properly.

- **Be aware of other ways to get into your estat lishment.** This can include roofs, basements an fire escapes.

- **Install an alarm system.** Alarm systems typica wire all entry points, and many provide motion detectors as well. These systems can activate on site alarms, or they can be connected to your lo police station.

- **Lighting.** Make sure you have adequate lighting inside and outside your facility.

- **Customer theft.** Customers are also sources of external theft. Teach your employees to watch for change scams and credit card fraud.

- **Opening/closing times.** Make sure you have opening and closing policies in place.

- **Cash drop.** Make sure an employee does not make a nighttime cash drop alone.

- **Closing time.** Have closing employees recheck all doors before they leave.

- **Teamwork.** Don't let an employee work a shift alone.

- **Lock up.** Make sure that employees lock the restaurant's doors after the last customer has left.

- **Employee safety.** Remember, you also need to keep your employees safe. Provide them with a plan for what to do if a robbery occurs while they are on the premises. Check with your local police department for suggestions on how to handle robberies, and make this information available to all employees.

Be sure to review your menu and update as needed.

CHAPTER EIGHT

FINAL TASKS

Life Cycle of Menu Items

Many menu items have a life cycle. This cycle includes a period of introduction, a period of popularity and a period of decline. You need to be able to identify and move with this cycle. Recognize the following:

- **Trends.** As an industry, the restaurant business must be aware of current food trends. But, because something is a trend it will, by definition, change. Right now, for instance, one of the trends is comfort food. Recently one of the food trends was fusion cuisine. Always keep up to date with such trends. Subscribe to trade journals and several consumer food and cooking magazines.

- **Review.** Because trends change, you need to review your menu periodically. There are likely to be items that are no longer popular. Consider taking them off your menu and replacing them with something more likely to sell.

- **Competition.** Never become complacent. Shop the competition, regularly, for new ideas for your menu.

Raising Prices

At some point in your career as a food service manager, you have to deal with the issue of raising prices. When you are designing, always consider the following pricing issues:

- **Reasons for raising prices.** Take an overall review of your establishment. You may be experiencing higher food costs because food prices have risen significantly since your last price review. Perhaps you have just undergone major renovation and have upgraded the atmosphere of your restaurant. Competition may have changed since the last increase. Or, you may have decided that you need to make a bigger profit in order for it to be worthwhile to stay in business. All of these are valid reasons for price increases. The way to implement increases, however, should be considered carefully.

- **Target certain items first.** If you do an across-the-board price increase, you may scare off some customers. You may want to consider increasing the price on a certain number of key dishes and leaving other price increases for a later date.

- **Decide how to communicate these increases.** Should you print a new menu or devise a way to increase the price on existing copies of the menu It's never a good idea to simply cross out the old price and write in the new. However, many food service managers also feel that it is a bad idea to increase prices when you print new menus that have changes in the items being offered. Whatever you decide, don't alert customers to pr increases!

- **Test market?** It may be best to reprint old menus with new prices and save any changes to the bill of fare until a later printing. This strategy will also let you "test market" the new prices. If you're not seeing the sales you need from the new prices, you can adjust them with a second printing.

aluating Your Work

fter all your hard work, don't miss this last crucial
step of menu planning. Take the time to analyze
w your sales and profits have been affected (or
affected) by your new menu. Review your overall
formance:

- **Employee involvement.** Take a look at your sales history, production sheets and menu sales analysis. Ask your employees what customers have been saying, and see if the new menu is allowing you to attain your target food cost.

- **Ask your customers directly.** When you put a new menu in place or when you change an existing menu drastically, develop a comment card and have your servers ask customers to fill it out. After all, the customers are the final menu test!

INDEX